D1462770

Celebrate
with
Cupcakes

Celebrate
with
Cupcakes

D&C

David and Charles

www.bakeme.com

A DAVID & CHARLES BOOK
© F&W Media International, LTD 2012

David & Charles is an imprint of F&W Media International, LTD
Brunel House, Forde Close, Newton Abbot, TQ12 4PU, UK

F&W Media International, LTD is a subsidiary of F+W Media, Inc.
4700 East Galbraith Road, Cincinnati, OH 45236

First published in the UK & US in 2012

Text and designs copyright © Lindy Smith 2012
Photography and illustrations © F&W Media International, LTD 2012

Lindy Smith has asserted her right to be identified as author of this work in accordance with the Copyright, Designs
and Patents Act, 1988.

All rights reserved. No part of this publication may be reproduced, stored in a retrieval system, or transmitted,
in any form or by any means, electronic or mechanical, by photocopying, recording or otherwise, without prior
permission in writing from the publisher.

Readers are permitted to reproduce any of the patterns or designs in this book for their personal use and without the
prior permission of the publisher. However the designs in this book are copyright and must not be reproduced for resale.

The author and publisher have made every effort to ensure that all the instructions in the book are accurate and safe,
and therefore cannot accept liability for any resulting injury, damage or loss to persons or property, however it may arise.

Names of manufacturers, products and product ranges are provided for the information of readers, with no intention
to infringe copyright or trademarks.

A catalogue record for this book is available from the British Library.

ISBN-13: 978-1-4463-0054-1 paperback
ISBN-10: 1-4463-0054-4 paperback

Printed in China by RR Donnelley
for F&W Media International LTD,
Brunel House, Forde Close, Newton Abbot, TQ12 4PU, UK

10 9 8 7 6 5 4 3 2 1

Publisher Alison Myer
Acquisitions Editor Jennifer Fox-Proverbs
Desk Editor Jeni Hennah
Assistant Editor Grace Harvey
Project Editor Jo Richardson
Creative Manager Prudence Rogers
Senior Production Controller Kelly Smith
Photography Karl Adamson and Sian Irvine
F+W Media publishes high quality books on a wide range
of subjects. For more great book ideas visit: www.rucraft.co.uk

Contents

Introduction

Cupcakes – what could be better cakes to bake? Lots of flavours, quick to bake, easy to ice and such a treat to eat. Known as fairy cakes during my childhood, cupcakes first became popular over 200 years ago as afternoon tea became fashionable, and delicacy and refinement were the order of the day. Today cupcakes are enjoying a well-deserved resurgence in their popularity. But no longer are they just small, light and tasty sponge cakes – they have been reinvented with a myriad of flavoured toppings, icings and eye-catching decorations.

The cupcakes in this book are all taken from three of my previous titles. Each cupcake is decorated to complement larger cakes from these books, so all are relatively easy to re-create. Simply choose a recipe to bake, a topping to add flavour and then design to add the final pizzazz.

I adore baking and decorating cupcakes, and I hope that by using this book you will also fall in love, if you haven't already, with making these small edible treats. Try experimenting with recipes, then share your results with family and friends – nothing could be more satisfying!

Have fun!

Lindy

www.lindyscakes.co.uk

Visit the Lindy's Cakes blog for more recipe ideas

How to use this book

The following reference section presents a couple of cupcake recipes plus variations, as well as introducing you to some of the basic techniques for icing and decorating. The projects use a variety of equipment, and the most frequently used are listed in the Basic Equipment section. Where particular makes of cutters or decorations are specified in the projects, you will find an abbreviation for the name of the supplier in brackets. Please refer to the abbreviations list with the suppliers details (see Suppliers).

Each individual cupcake project details all the various items of equipment you will need, together with materials required, such as the different types of icing, paste colours and dusts. These can be obtained from cake-decorating stores or online stockists – again, see Suppliers for contact details. A few templates are also provided to help you create the cupcake decorations (see Templates).

Basic equipment

The following is a list of items of equipment that have been frequently used for the projects in this book. A key to the abbreviations and details of suppliers can be found under Suppliers.

Cocktail stick (toothpick), used as a marker and to transfer small amounts of paste colour (**1**)

Cutters come in various shapes and sizes for cutting out and embossing shapes (**2**)

Foam pad (PME) creates a surface on which to thin flower petals (**3**)

Measuring spoons for accurate measurement of ingredients (**4**)

Moulds, daisy centre stamps (JEM), used for creating flower centres (**5**)

Multi-ribbon cutter (FMM), a time-saving tool for cutting strips of paste (**6**)

Paintbrushes for stippling, painting and dusting

Paint palette for mixing paste colours and dusts prior to painting

Palette knife for cutting paste (**7**)

Piping tubes (tips) used for piping royal icing and cutting out small circles (**8**)

Reusable piping bag and coupler to hold royal icing for piping (**9**)

Rolling pin for rolling out different types of paste

Scissors for cutting templates and trimming paste to shape (**10**)

Smoother for helping to create a smooth and even finish to sugarpaste (rolled fondant) (**11**)

Spacers, narrow and 5mm (³⁄₁₆in), for rolling out paste

Stick embossers (HP), small embosser used to add patterns to paste (**12**)

Sugar shaper and discs to create pieces of uniformly shaped modelling paste (**13**)

Tools:
• Ball tool (FMM) gives even indentations in paste and softens the edges of petals (**14**)
• Dresden tool (FMM) for creating markings on paste (**15**)
• Cutting wheel (PME) for using instead of a knife to avoid dragging the paste (**16**)
• Scriber (PME) for scribing around templates (**17**)
• Craft knife for intricate cutting tasks (**18**)

Work board, non-stick, used for rolling out pastes (**19**)

Cupcake pans

There are standard- and mini-sized cupcake (muffin) pans available, and both types can vary in size. The cup shape also varies – generally, the more angled the sides, the more surface you have for decorating.

Cupcake cases

It is important that the cases fit snugly inside the pans to ensure they are supported during baking. Standard thin, supermarket-style cases turn translucent when baked. This can detract from a patterned case, so use a double or triple layer, or spend a little more and buy foil-covered cases or thicker paper ones.

Cupcake pans and cases are essentials for baking, along with cutters and piping tubes (tips) for decorating.

Piping tubes

These are the main sizes available. Tube numbers vary with suppliers, so always check the diameter.

Tube No. (PME)	Diameter
0	0.5mm (0.020in)
1	1mm (^{1}⁄₃₂in)
1.5	1.2mm (^{1}⁄₃₂in)
2	1.5mm (^{1}⁄₁₆in)
3	2mm (^{3}⁄₃₂in)
4	3mm (^{1}⁄₈in)
16	5mm (^{3}⁄₁₆in)
17	6mm (^{1}⁄₄in)
18	7mm (^{1}⁄₄in)

US cup measurements

If you prefer to use cup measurements, please use the following conversions. (Note: 1 Australian tbsp = 20ml.)

liquid 1 tsp = 5ml; 1 tbsp = 15ml; ½ cup = 120ml/4fl oz; 1 cup = 240ml/8½fl oz

butter 1 tbsp = 15g/½oz; 2 tbsp = 25g/1oz; ½ cup/1 stick = 115g/4oz; 1 cup/2 sticks = 225g/8oz

caster (superfine) sugar/brown sugar ½ cup = 100g/3½oz; 1 cup = 200g/7oz

icing (confectioners') sugar 1 cup = 115g/4oz

flour 1 cup = 140g/5oz

desiccated (dry unsweetened shredded) coconut 1 cup = 90g/3¼oz

sultanas (golden raisins) 165g/5¾oz

Baking cupcakes

Baking cupcakes should be fun! First of all, choose your cupcake cases and then select a recipe to use. The two cupcake recipes in this book are included to get you off to a good start, but any cake recipe will usually work, so please don't be afraid to experiment with flavours. Further tried and thoroughly tested cupcake recipes can be found in my *Bake Me I'm Yours… Cupcake Celebration* book and on the Lindy's Cakes blog.

Lemon cupcakes

Makes approx. 24

Ingredients
- 250g (9oz) unsalted butter, softened
- 250g (9oz) caster (superfine) sugar
- 250g (9oz) self-raising (-rising) flour, sifted
- 4 large free-range eggs, at room temperature
- finely grated zest of 2 lemons
- 60ml (4 tbsp) freshly squeezed lemon juice

1 Preheat the oven to 170°C/325°F/Gas 3. Line 24 holes of bun trays (muffin pans) with paper cupcake cases.

2 Beat the butter and sugar together in a large mixing bowl until light, fluffy and very pale. Add the remaining ingredients and beat until the mixture is smooth.

3 Fill the paper cases half-full with the mixture, using either a spoon or a piping bag (A).

4 Bake for about 20 minutes, or until the tops of the cakes spring back when lightly touched or a fine skewer inserted into the centre comes out clean. Leave to cool for a couple of minutes before removing to a wire rack to cool completely (B).

Chocolate cupcakes

Makes approx. 24

Ingredients
- 120g (4¼oz) good-quality dark (bittersweet or semisweet) chocolate, broken into pieces
- 250ml (9fl oz) water
- 180g (6½ oz) butter, cut into cubes
- 220g (8oz) caster (superfine) sugar
- 4 large free-range eggs, at room temperature
- 200g (7oz) self-raising (-rising) flour
- 4 tbsp cocoa powder (unsweetened cocoa)
- 80g (3oz) ground almonds

1 Preheat the oven to 170°C/325°F/Gas 3. Line 24 holes of bun trays (muffin pans) with paper cupcake cases.

2 Place the chocolate, water, butter and sugar into a large saucepan and warm over a low heat, stirring frequently, until the chocolate and butter have melted. Leave to cool, then beat in the eggs.

3 Sift the flour, cocoa and ground almonds into a large mixing bowl and make a well in the centre. Gradually pour the chocolate mixture into the well and beat with a wooden spoon until combined.

4 Pour the mixture into the paper cases until about three-quarters full. Bake for about 30 minutes, or until a fine skewer inserted into the centre comes out clean. Leave to cool for a couple of minutes before removing to a wire rack to cool completely.

Flavour variations
Raspberry and chocolate Add 200g (7oz) fresh or frozen raspberries
Chocolate orange Add the finely grated zest of 1 orange

Other flavoured cupcakes

Use the recipe for Lemon Cupcakes but replace the lemon zest and juice with one of the following options:

- **Orange** Finely grated zest of 1 orange and 60ml (4 tbsp) orange juice
- **Vanilla** 5ml (1 tsp) vanilla extract and 60ml (4 tbsp) milk
- **Chocolate chip** 200g (7oz) chocolate chips and 60ml (4 tbsp) milk
- **Boozy** Use Madeira or Baileys in place of some of the liquid, the exact quantity depending on your preference, and make up the balance with milk
- **Lavender** 4 tbsp organic dried lavender flowers and 60ml (4 tbsp) milk
- **Strawberry jam** 60ml (4 tbsp) milk, then swirl 1 tsp jam through the cake mixture in each paper case before baking
- **Rose** 30ml (2 tbsp) rosewater and 30ml (2 tbsp) milk
- **Asian delight** 50g (1¾oz) flaked almonds, 1 tbsp crushed fennel seeds, 2 tsp ground cardamom, 5ml (2 tsp) almond extract and 60ml (4 tbsp) milk

Sugar recipes

Most of the sugar recipes used in this book for covering, modelling and decoration can easily be made at home. Use paste colours to colour them according to the individual project.

Sugarpaste

Ready-made sugarpaste (rolled fondant) is available from supermarkets and cake-decorating suppliers in various colours. It is also easy and inexpensive to make your own.

Makes 1kg (2¼lb)

Ingredients
• 60ml (4 tbsp) cold water
• 4 tsp/1 sachet powdered gelatine
• 125ml (4fl oz) liquid glucose
• 15ml (1 tbsp) glycerine
• 1kg (2¼lb) icing (confectioners') sugar, sifted, plus extra for dusting

1 Place the water in a small bowl, sprinkle over the gelatine and leave to soak until spongy. Stand the bowl over a saucepan of hot but not boiling water and stir until the gelatine is dissolved. Add the glucose and glycerine, stirring until well blended and runny.

2 Put the icing sugar in a large bowl, make a well in the centre and slowly pour in the liquid ingredients, stirring constantly. Mix well. Turn out onto a surface dusted with icing sugar and knead until smooth, sprinkling with extra icing sugar if the paste becomes too sticky. The paste can be used immediately or tightly wrapped and stored in a plastic bag.

tip

For tips and discussion about making your own sugarpaste, please visit the Lindy's Cakes blog.

By using discs of sugarpaste in soft pastel shades, these cupcakes have a fresh, feminine appeal.

Modelling paste

This versatile paste keeps its shape well, dries harder than sugarpaste (rolled fondant) and is used for adding decorations to cupcakes. If time is short, use CMC (Tylose) instead of gum tragacanth, a synthetic product that works almost straight away.

Makes 225g (8oz)

Ingredients
• 1 tsp gum tragacanth
• 225g (8oz) sugarpaste (rolled fondant)

Add the gum tragacanth to the sugarpaste and knead in. Wrap in a plastic bag and allow the gum to work before use. You will begin to feel a difference in the paste after an hour or so, but it is best left overnight. The modelling paste should be firm but pliable with a slightly elastic texture. Kneading the modelling paste makes it warm and easy to work with.

This beautiful rosebud decoration is formed from a folded and rolled-up strip of modelling paste to resemble a fabric flower.

Pastillage

Pastillage is extremely useful because, unlike modelling paste, it sets extremely hard and is not affected by moisture. However, the paste crusts quickly and is brittle once dry. You can also buy pastillage in a powdered form, to which you add water.

Makes 1kg (2¼lb)

Ingredients
• 1 medium free-range egg white
• 300g (10½oz) icing (confectioners') sugar, sifted
• 2 tsp gum tragacanth

1 Put the egg white in a large mixing bowl. Gradually add enough icing sugar until the mixture combines together into a ball. Mix in the gum tragacanth, then turn the paste out onto a work surface and knead the pastillage well.

2 Incorporate the remaining icing sugar into the rest of the pastillage to give a stiff paste. Store in a plastic bag in an airtight container in a refrigerator for up to one month.

This amazingly realistic butterfly has been formed from pastillage using a commercial mould and then painted with paste colours diluted with clear spirit.

Chocolate ganache

A must for all chocoholics, use the best chocolate
you can source for a really indulgent topping.

Ingredients

Dark chocolate ganache:
• 200g (7oz) dark (bittersweet or semisweet) chocolate,
broken into pieces
• 200ml (7fl oz) double (heavy) cream

White chocolate ganache:
• 600g (1lb 5oz) white chocolate, broken into pieces
• 80ml (21/2fl oz) double (heavy) cream

1 Melt the chocolate and cream together in a heatproof bowl.
set over a saucepan of gently simmering water, stirring
to combine. Alternatively, melt in a microwave on low power,
stirring every 20 seconds or so.

2 The ganache can be used warm once it has thickened
slightly and is of a pouring consistency, or it can be left to
cool so that it can be spread with a palette knife. Alternatively,
once completely cool, it can be whisked to give a lighter texture.

Royal icing

Ingredients
• 1 medium free-range egg white
• 250g (9oz) icing (confectioners') sugar, sifted

Put the egg white into a bowl and gradually beat in the icing
sugar until the icing is glossy and forms soft peaks.

Sugar syrup

This simple syrup can also be infused with flavours to add a
unique twist, such as vanilla pods, cardamom seeds and root
ginger, or simply use Demerara sugar (raw brown sugar) instead
of white sugar to give a richer flavour.

Ingredients
• 250ml (9fl oz) water
• 250g (9oz) caster (superfine) sugar

1 Bring to the boil in a saucepan and stir until the sugar has
dissolved – don't boil for too long, or it will be too thick.

Sugar glue

This is a quick, easy instant glue to make and my preferred
choice. Break up pieces of white modelling paste into a small
container and cover with boiling water. Stir until dissolved
or place in a microwave for 10 seconds before stirring. This
produces a thick, strong glue that can be easily thinned by
adding more cooled boiled water. For a stronger glue, use
pastillage as the base instead, useful for delicate work.

*The arty background effect on this sophisticated
cupcake has been created by using swirled and
textured gold-tinted royal icing.*

These cute little curly fleeced sheep have been piped onto the sugarpaste topping using tinted buttercream.

Buttercream

A very versatile and popular topping for cupcakes, used on its own or to pipe decoration onto sugarpaste, or spread under a disc of coloured sugarpaste.

Ingredients
• 110g (3¾oz) unsalted butter, softened
• 350g (12oz) icing (confectioners') sugar
• 15–30ml (1–2 tbsp) milk or water
• a few drops of vanilla extract or alternative flavouring

1 Beat the butter in a bowl until light and fluffy. Sift in the sugar and beat until the mixture changes colour. Add just enough milk or water to give a firm but spreadable consistency.

2 Flavour by adding the vanilla or alternative flavouring (see below), then store in an airtight container until required.

Flavouring buttercream
Try replacing the liquid in the recipe with:
* Alcohols such as whisky, rum or brandy
* Other liquids such as coffee, lemon curd, or fresh fruit purées
Or add:
* Nut butters to make a praline flavour
* Flavourings such as mint or rose extract

Chocolate buttercream
Mix 2 tbsp cocoa powder (unsweetened cocoa) with the liquid before adding to the beaten mixture. Omit the flavourings.

White chocolate buttercream
Ingredients
• 115g (4oz) white chocolate, broken into pieces
• 225g (8oz) icing (confectioners') sugar
• 115g (4oz) unsalted butter, softened

Melt the white chocolate in a bowl set over a saucepan of gently simmering water and leave to cool slightly. Beat the icing sugar into the butter, then beat in the melted chocolate.

Confectioners' glaze

This is used when a glossy-looking sheen is needed and where a surface needs sealing, available from cake-decorating suppliers.

White vegetable fat

This solid vegetable fat (shortening) is sold under different brand names: in the UK, Trex or White Flora; in the USA, Crisco; in Australia, Copha; and in South Africa, Holsum. These products are more or less interchangeable in cake making.

Edible glitter

Please make sure when adding glitter to your cupcakes that you use edible glitter, not glitter labelled as non-toxic, which is often sold alongside edible products. If you would like to make your own edible glitter, visit Lindy's Cakes blog.

tip

For a diary-free buttercream, replace the butter with solid white vegetable fat (shortening).

Decorating cupcakes

It is worth doing a little preparation before covering your cupcakes. Not all cupcakes come out of the oven perfect – some may need a little trimming with a sharp knife, while others could benefit from building up with an appropriate icing. First, check each of your cupcakes to ensure that the decoration is going to sit just as you want and remedy any that aren't quite right.

1 The sugarpaste may need a little help to secure it to the cupcakes, so brush the cakes with an appropriate syrup (see Sugar Syrup) or alcohol, or add a thin layer of buttercream or ganache (see Sugar Recipes), which also adds flavour and interest to the cake.

2 Knead the sugarpaste until warm and pliable. Roll out on a surface lightly smeared with white vegetable fat (shortening), rather than icing sugar, to a depth of 5mm (³⁄₁₆in). It is a good idea to use spacers, as they ensure an even thickness (A).

3 Cut out circles of sugarpaste using an appropriately sized cutter (B). The size of the circle required will be dependent on the cupcake pan and case used and the amount that the cakes have domed.

4 Carefully lift the paste circles onto each cupcake with a palette knife (C), then use the palm of your hand to shape the paste to the cupcake, easing the fullness in if necessary.

Painting techniques

Many fabulous effects can be achieved by painting over dried sugarpaste (rolled fondant). Painting also helps to brighten the overall appearance of your cupcakes, as even vividly coloured paste will dry to a dull finish.

Food colours behave in much the same way as ordinary water-based paints, so you can mix and blend them to produce many different tones and hues (see Colouring Paste). To paint sugarpaste, dilute some paste colour with clear spirit such as gin or vodka and, using a paintbrush, a damp natural sponge or a stippling brush, apply to the dry sugarpaste. For deep colours, add a little clear spirit to some paste colour. For light colours, or if you want to apply a colour wash, add a little colour to some clear spirit.

A stippling brush will give a subtle effect when used to paint sugarpaste (rolled fondant).

Use a fine paintbrush to add intricate detail, such as animal or insect markings.

Colouring paste

Sugarpaste (rolled fondant) and modelling paste are now available in all kinds of bright colours. However, if you can't find the exact colour you are looking for, or if only a small amount of a colour is required, it is often best to colour your own paste or adjust the colour of a commercial paste. The basic colour-mixing diagram below will give you a quick reference point for mixing paste colours. Depending on the amount of paste you wish to colour and the depth of colour required, place a little paste colour (don't use liquid colour) on the end of a cocktail stick (toothpick) or a larger amount onto the end of a palette knife. Add to the paste and knead in thoroughly, adding more until you have the desired result. Be careful with pale colours, as only a little colour is needed. Deep colours, on the other hand, require plenty and will become quite sticky.

To overcome this, add a pinch of gum tragacanth and leave for an hour or two; the gum will make the paste firmer and easier to handle. Note: the coloured paste will appear slightly darker when dry.

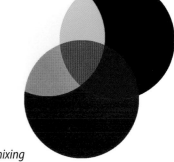

Basic colour mixing

Making moulds

The Terrific Tortoises and the Tiger Treats projects both use moulded animals as decorations. Commercial moulds tend to be expensive and are often not exactly what you require, but it's quite easy to make your own instead.

Making and using a mould

you will need

- non-toxic modelling clay or Plasticine, available from toy and art stores or online suppliers
- Dresden tool and cutting wheel
- pot of moulding gel
- modelling paste
- edible paste colours
- clear spirit, such as gin or vodka
- paintbrushes

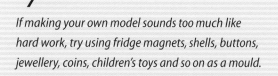

tip

If making your own model sounds too much like hard work, try using fridge magnets, shells, buttons, jewellery, coins, children's toys and so on as a mould.

1 To make the original model to be moulded, knead some modelling clay to warm it and build up the basic design using rolled shapes, then blend and texture as appropriate. Make the model with a flat base. The picture (A) shows how the tiger's head has been built up from a half-ball shape by adding sausage and ball shapes, blended with a Dresden tool and textured with a cutting wheel.

A

2 Roll out some modelling clay, not too thinly, place the model in the centre and then bring up the sides and pinch them together to form a container. Alternatively, you can make a container from some aluminium foil, or use a plastic beaker or small bowl.

3 Melt the moulding gel following the manufacturer's instructions on the pot, and then pour it into the container until the model is completely covered (B).

6 Once the moulded shapes are dry, dilute some paste colours in clear spirit and then paint as appropriate (D).

4 Leave until set (usually 5–10 minutes) and then carefully peel away the container. Turn the mould upside down and carefully remove the model from the base of the mould.

5 Knead some modelling paste to warm it and roll it into a ball. Press the ball firmly into the newly created mould, level the paste with the top of the mould and then carefully release (C). Repeat to make as many shapes as you need.

tip

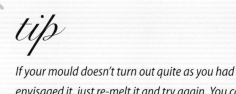

If your mould doesn't turn out quite as you had envisaged it, just re-melt it and try again. You can also reuse the gel after you have finished making a set of models with it.

Decorations, storage, transportation and display

It is a good idea to invest in a few ready-made decorations to help jazz up your cupcakes. Remember to store your final creations carefully to ensure that they remain in perfect condition before they are served. As you want your cupcakes to look their best, plan ahead and consider how you will display them to their best advantage.

Edible decorations

There is an ever-increasing variety of ready-made decorations available from supermarkets and sugarcraft suppliers, and they are a great way of saving time and adding that extra touch when used wisely. Dragées (sugar balls) are particularly attractive and feature in a number of projects in this book, as they add a touch of glamour and opulence to the cakes.

Storing cupcakes

Once your cupcakes have cooled, store them in an airtight container at room temperature until you are ready to decorate them. Decorate your cupcakes as close as possible to when they are to be eaten, to help prevent them from drying out.

tip

If you aren't able to decorate your cupcakes just before serving, use foil or high-quality greaseproof cases and cover the whole of the top of the cakes to help seal in the moisture.

Transporting cupcakes

Cardboard cupcake boxes are the best way to transport precious cupcakes – they are simply cardboard boxes with an insert. Pop the cupcakes into the insert to prevent the cakes from sliding about. You can even then stack the boxes so that the cupcakes are easy to carry. Boxes are available for the different case sizes and range from single-hole boxes to at least 24 holes.

Displaying cupcakes

Give your cupcakes an extra wow factor by displaying them on a stand especially designed for the purpose. Alternatively, place your cupcakes on a pretty plate stand and decorate with ribbons and fresh flowers to complement the colours and designs that you have used on your cupcakes.

Bring on the bling!

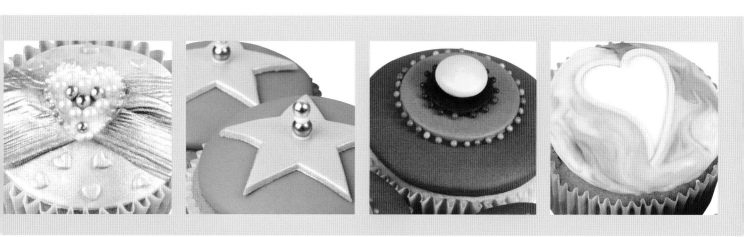

We all love to throw caution to the wind now and again and indulge in the heady heights of decadence. And that more often than not means all that glitters, glows or sparkles. The excuse for such decorative excess doesn't have to be limited to the annual festive frenzy of Christmas time. Valentine's Day, a special birthday or a wedding anniversary – including of course the major Silver and Golden milestones – are all ideal times to bring on the bling.

Here we have an eclectic range of cupcake schemes that are guaranteed to dazzle and delight, some by way of their dramatic colours and bold motifs, others in the more traditional guise of gold and silver sugar decorations and sparkle dusts. Either way, these are cupcakes purpose-designed to grab the attention and create a stir.

Paisley, pearls 'n' swirls

This sophisticated cupcake collection offers a rich tapestry of colour and pattern, with metallic sugar balls and a dusting of sparkle providing eye-catching highlights. But these fabulous effects are surprisingly easy to achieve using simple cut-out shapes and swirls created with a sugar shaper tool.

An extra dimension is brought to the designs by giving the base sugarpaste a decorative paint treatment using diluted paste colours applied with a stippling brush for a textured look. You can incorporate these simple, speedy techniques in all sorts of cupcake decorating schemes, to give them a creative edge.

you will need ...

materials

- 24 vanilla or other flavoured cupcakes, or chocolate cupcakes
- sugarpaste (rolled fondant): burgundy, red, pink, orange
- gum tragacanth
- paste colours: burgundy, red, pink
- clear spirit, such as gin or vodka
- 4mm (⅛in) gold and silver dragées (sugar balls)
- mulberry sparkle dust
- white vegetable fat (shortening)
- sugar glue

equipment

- non-stick work board
- rolling pin
- 5mm (³⁄₁₆in) spacers
- flat-headed and fine paintbrushes; stippling brush
- kitchen paper (paper towels)
- cutters: circle cutter same diameter as top of cupcakes; Elegant Heart cutters (LC) 2.8cm (1¹⁄₁₆in), 2cm (¾in); paisley cutters (LC)
- narrow spacers made from 1.5mm (¹⁄₁₆in) thick card
- sugar shaper with small round disc
- craft knife
- no. 18 piping tube (tip)

Making the cupcakes

Make and bake your chosen flavour of cupcakes
(see Baking Cupcakes for recipes).

Preparing the cupcakes

1 Brush the cakes with syrup or alcohol or add a thin layer of buttercream or ganache (see Sugar Recipes), to help keep them fresh and to help the sugarpaste stick to the cakes.

2 Knead each of the sugarpaste colours to warm, then roll out between the 5mm (³⁄₁₆in) spacers, ideally on a non-stick surface. Using a circle cutter of the appropriate size, cut 12 red, six pink and six burgundy sugarpaste circles. Using a palette knife, carefully lift each paste circle onto a cupcake.

Applying the background paint effects

1 Dilute some burgundy, red and pink paste colours with clear spirit.

2 Take the stippling brush and stipple burgundy paste colour over the burgundy sugarpaste circles, red paste colour over the red sugarpaste circles and pink paste colour over the pink sugarpaste circles to intensify the colours and create a textured look (A). Leave to dry.

A

Making the heart design

1 Roll out the pink and burgundy modelling pastes between the narrow spacers, then cut out six pink hearts using the larger heart cutter. Cut out 12 burgundy hearts using the smaller heart cutter. Attach one larger pink heart to each of the pink stippled cupcakes, with the two smaller burgundy hearts, inverted, either side and below.

2 Stipple the hearts using the appropriate diluted paste colour, then attach a silver dragée to the tip of each small heart. Once the paint has partially dried but is tacky, dust over the hearts with some edible glitter.

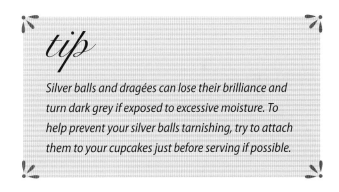

tip

Silver balls and dragées can lose their brilliance and turn dark grey if exposed to excessive moisture. To help prevent your silver balls tarnishing, try to attach them to your cupcakes just before serving if possible.

Making the paisley design

1 Roll out the orange and burgundy modelling pastes using the narrow spacers. Use the two smallest paisley cutters to cut out some paisley shapes from each colour. Arrange one larger orange and one larger burgundy shape on each red stippled cupcake, then add a smaller contrasting-coloured shape to one of each pair.

2 Soften some of the burgundy modelling paste by kneading in a little white vegetable fat and then partially dunking the paste into a small container of boiled water before kneading again – the paste should have the consistency of chewing gum. Place the paste with the small round disc into the sugar shaper. Paint sugar glue around the larger orange paisley shapes, adding a curl to the end of each. Squeeze out lengths of paste and place over the glue, cutting to size with a craft knife. Repeat with the orange modelling paste around the burgundy shapes.

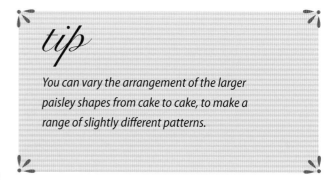

tip

You can vary the arrangement of the larger paisley shapes from cake to cake, to make a range of slightly different patterns.

3 Roll out the red and burgundy modelling pastes using the narrow spacers and cut out small circles using the no. 18 piping tube. Attach the red circles to the larger paisley shapes without the small paisley shapes and the burgundy circles to spaces on some of the cupcakes.

Making the swirl design

1 Using a fine paintbrush, paint sugar glue swirls onto the burgundy-covered cupcakes.

2 Soften some of the orange modelling paste. Place with the small round disc into the sugar shaper. Squeeze out lengths of paste and place over the glue, cutting to size with a craft knife.

The finishing touch

Dilute some of the paste colours with clear spirit and paint over areas of the cupcake decorations, such as parts of the paisley shapes, swirls and pink hearts, to enhance their look (C). Add gold dragées to the centre of some of the small circles and the paisley shapes.

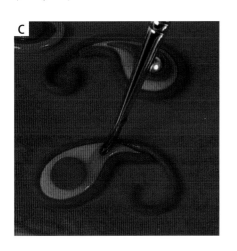

C

tip

For tips and discussion on using a sugar shaper, please visit the Lindy's Cakes blog.

Status Symbols

These designer cupcakes with their boldly contrasting colours and geometric-shaped decorations make a real style statement. But it's a cutting-edge look that's easy to achieve using just two cutters and simple painting techniques.

The blue of the sugarpaste discs is given extra intensity and interest by being stippled with blue paste colour. An element of glitz is then added by gilding the modelling paste circles set within the triangles. Also included is a variation on the main motif – a dazzling blue and gold-glazed Eastern-inspired star.

you will need ...

materials

- 24 lemon or other flavoured cupcakes, or chocolate cupcakes
- complementary flavour of syrup, alcohol, buttercream or ganache
- 650g (1lb 7oz) blue sugarpaste (rolled fondant)
- blue paste colour
- clear spirit, such as gin or vodka
- modelling paste: 100g (3½oz) each gold and ivory
- edible gold lustre dust
- confectioners' glaze
- sugar glue (see Sugar Recipes)

equipment

- non-stick work board
- large and small rolling pin
- 5mm (³⁄₁₆in) spacers
- cutters: circles – same diameter as top of cupcakes and 1.5cm (⅝in); equilateral triangle, side measurements 3.25cm (1¼in)
- palette knife
- stippling brush and fine flat-headed paintbrush
- narrow spacers made from 1.5mm (¹⁄₁₆in) thick card
- waxed paper

Making and preparing the cupcakes

1 Make and bake your chosen flavour of cupcakes (see Baking Cupcakes for recipes).

2 Brush the cakes with syrup or alcohol or add a thin layer of buttercream or ganache (see Sugar Recipes), to help keep them fresh and to help the sugarpaste stick to the cakes.

3 Knead the sugarpaste to warm, then roll out between the 5mm (³⁄₁₆in) spacers, ideally on a non-stick surface. Cut out 24 circles using a circle cutter of the appropriate size. Using a palette knife, carefully lift each paste circle onto a cupcake.

Painting the background discs

Dilute the blue paste colour with clear spirit. Use the stippling brush to stipple over the covered cakes (A).

Making the triangle decorations

1 Roll out the gold modelling paste between the narrow spacers. Use the 1.5cm (⅝in) circle cutter to cut out 24 circles. Place the circles on a sheet of waxed paper. Mix edible gold lustre dust with some confectioners' glaze and, while the circles are still soft, use the flat-headed paintbrush to paint them with the gold glaze.

2 Roll out the ivory modelling paste between the narrow spacers. Use the triangle cutter to cut out 24 triangles.

3 While they are still soft, attach a gilded circle to the centre of each ivory triangle, then attach one triangle to the centre of each cupcake with sugar glue (B).

Star Signs

For a more decorative finish, try making these pretty star designs instead of the simple triangles.

1 As an alternative to the triangle decorations, roll out blue modelling paste between the narrow spacers and use the 1.5cm (⅝in) cutter to cut out 24 circles. Roll out gold modelling paste in the same way and use two long teardrop cutters in two sizes, 2.25cm (⅞in) and 1.75cm (¾in), to cut out four larger and four smaller teardrops for each cupcake.

2 Place a blue circle on waxed paper and arrange the teardrops, alternating in size, around it. Take a 2cm (¾in) square cutter and place it centrally over the circle, adjusting the position of the teardrops as necessary. Press down on the cutter, then remove the small pieces of excess paste in the middle (A). Make 23 more stars in the same way and leave to dry.

3 Paint the points of the stars with the gold glaze, as for the triangle decorations (B), to gild them. Attach a blue circle to the centre of each cupcake, then arrange the points in position around the circles.

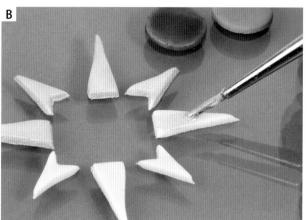

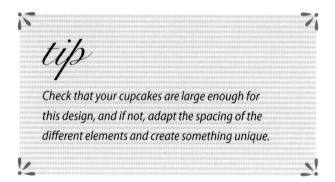

tip

Check that your cupcakes are large enough for this design, and if not, adapt the spacing of the different elements and create something unique.

Crowning Glory

These cupcakes are fit for any budding princess or prince, with their dazzling golden crowns encrusted with decorative detailing. They couldn't, however, be easier to create, using a cutter or the template provided (see Templates) to cut out the basic crown shapes and simple piping techniques to add the decoration.

The splendid gold finish is also quick and easy to achieve by first coating the crown with white vegetable fat and then brushing over edible gold lustre dust.

you will need . . .

materials

- 24 lemon or other flavoured cupcakes, or chocolate cupcakes
- complementary flavour of syrup, alcohol, buttercream or ganache
- 650g (1lb 7oz) green sugarpaste (rolled fondant)
- 100g (3½oz) gold modelling paste
- sugar glue (see Sugar Recipes)
- 1 quantity of royal icing coloured gold (see Sugar Recipes)
- white vegetable fat (shortening)
- edible gold lustre dust

equipment

- large and small rolling pin
- 5mm (³⁄₁₆in) spacers
- circle cutter same diameter as top of cupcakes
- palette knife
- narrow spacers made from 1.5mm (¹⁄₁₆in) thick card
- craft knife or crown cutter (LC)
- piping (pastry) bags and coupler with nos. 1, 2 and 3 plain piping tubes (tips) (PME)
- paintbrushes

Making and preparing the cupcakes

1 Make and bake your chosen flavour of cupcakes (see Baking Cupcakes for recipes).

2 Brush the cakes with syrup or alcohol or add a thin layer of buttercream or ganache (see Sugar Recipes), to help keep them fresh and to help the sugarpaste stick to the cakes.

3 Knead the sugarpaste to warm, then roll out between the 5mm (³⁄₁₆in) spacers, ideally on a non-stick surface. Cut out 24 circles using a circle cutter of the appropriate size. Using a palette knife, carefully lift each paste circle onto a cupcake.

Making the crown decorations

1 Roll out the gold modelling paste using the narrow spacers. Use the crown template (see Templates) to cut out 24 crowns with a craft knife, then attach to each cupcake with sugar glue. Alternatively, use an appropriately sized crown cutter.

2 Place the gold royal icing in a piping bag fitted with a coupler and a no. 3 tube and pipe a row of large dots a short distance from the base of the crown and one to the tip of each point. Unscrew the coupler, replace with a no. 2 tube and add medium dots and a band across the base. Change to a no. 1 tube and pipe rows of small dots as shown. Leave to dry.

3 Brush white vegetable fat over each crown and then dust with edible gold lustre dust.

Heraldic Splendour

Conjure up the majesty, heroism and romance of the medieval knights
with this collection of regal-looking cupcakes, sporting shields with
handsome coats of arms – perfect for celebrating a boy's birthday party.

In fact, this is a great opportunity to get the children involved in researching
designs for the shields, either in reference books or on the internet,
and coming up with their own schemes in their favourite colours.

you will need …

materials

- 24 lemon or other flavoured cupcakes, or chocolate cupcakes
- complementary flavour of syrup, alcohol, buttercream or ganache
- 650g (1lb 7oz) red sugarpaste (rolled fondant)
- modelling paste: 50 g (1¾oz) each yellow, orange, green, white; 25g (1oz) each black and blue
- sugar glue (see Sugar Recipes)

equipment

- non-stick work board
- large and small rolling pin
- 5mm (³⁄₁₆in) spacers
- cutters: circle cutter same diameter as top of cupcakes; shield cutter (FMM); long triangle cutter (optional)
- narrow spacers made from 1.5mm (¹⁄₁₆in) thick card
- large plain piping tube (tip), for cutting small circles
- craft knife and ruler

Making and preparing the cupcakes

1 Make and bake your chosen flavour of cupcakes (see Baking Cupcakes for recipes).

2 Brush the cakes with syrup or alcohol or add a thin layer of buttercream or ganache (see Sugar Recipes), to help keep them fresh and to help the sugarpaste stick to the cakes.

3 Knead the sugarpaste to warm, then roll out between the 5mm (³⁄₁₆in) spacers, ideally on a non-stick surface. Cut out 24 circles using a circle cutter of the appropriate size. Using a palette knife, carefully lift each paste circle onto a cupcake.

Making the shields

1 Roll out the first four modelling paste colours between the narrow spacers. Use the shield cutter to cut out eight shields from each. Attach one to each cupcake with sugar glue.

2 Roll out the black modelling paste between the narrow spacers. Using a craft knife and ruler, cut out eight strips and attach across the yellow shields; trim to fit. Use the end of the large piping tube to cut 16 circles and position either side of each strip. Cut out eight stars and attach to the orange shields.

3 Using a craft knife or cutter, cut out eight long triangles from the remaining green modelling paste for the centres of the white shields; attach with sugar glue. Roll out the blue modelling paste and cut out eight strips for the green shields.

Ribbons and Romance

These unashamedly romantic cupcakes will create the appropriate mood
for a wedding, anniversary or Valentine's party, or prettily packaged
to match they would make a lovely gift to mark such an occasion.

The draped satin ribbon effect is created by first texturing rectangles of
modelling paste before softly gathering and sugar-gluing in place across
the sugarcraft discs. Both hearts are made using cutters, the focal one then
decorated with dragées to resemble a pearl-studded brooch. The entire decorated
discs are then finished with lustre dusts to give them an alluring sheen.

you will need ...

materials

- 24 vanilla or other flavoured cupcakes, or chocolate cupcakes
- complementary flavour of syrup, alcohol, buttercream or ganache
- 250g (9oz) white modelling paste
- dragées (sugar balls): pink, ivory
- sugar glue (Sugar Recipes)
- 650g (1lb 7oz) white sugarpaste (rolled fondant)
- white vegetable fat (shortening)
- edible lustre dust: pink, white

equipment

- non-stick work board
- large and small rolling pin
- narrow spacers made from 1.5mm (¹⁄₁₆in) thick card
- cutters: 2.5cm (1in) heart cutter (FMM); cutter same diameter as top of cupcakes; miniature heart cutter
- 5mm (³⁄₁₆in) spacers
- waxed paper
- textured rolling pin (HP Watermark Taffeta Pin)
- soft dusting brush

Making the cupcakes

Make and bake your chosen flavour of cupcakes
(see Baking Cupcakes for recipes).

Creating the hearts

Roll out some of the modelling paste using the narrow spacers.
Using the 2.5cm (1in) heart cutter, cut out 24 hearts. Decorate
the edges with small pink and ivory dragées, then the centre
with medium and large dragées.

Preparing the cupcakes

1 Brush the cakes with syrup or alcohol or add a thin layer of buttercream or ganache (see Sugar Recipes), to help keep them fresh and to help the sugarpaste stick to the cakes.

2 Knead the sugarpaste to warm, then roll out between the 5mm (³⁄₁₆in) spacers, ideally on a non-stick surface. Cut out 24 circles using a circle cutter of the appropriate size and place on waxed paper.

Adding the decoration

1 Roll out a large rectangle of modelling paste and texture it with the textured rolling pin (A). Cut out 24 rectangles slightly wider than the cupcakes. Pinch the centre of each rectangle to create a loose fabric effect, then attach one shaped rectangle across each sugarpaste circle with sugar glue. Next, attach the edges to the curved edge of each circle, trimming to fit if necessary.

2 Use a miniature heart cutter to cut out a selection of small hearts from the remaining thinly rolled-out modelling paste (B). Attach these above and below the fabric decoration on each circle of sugarpaste.

3 Brush the sugarpaste circles with white vegetable fat and, using a soft dusting brush, cover the decorated discs with your choice of edible lustre dusts.

4 Carefully add the decorated circles to the top of each cupcake and top with a decorated heart.

A

B

Hearts of Silver

Have a go at making these sparkly pink cupcakes for a little girl's birthday party, with sugarpaste flowers and silver heart decorations.

1 Roll out some deep pink and pale pink sugarpaste to a thickness of 5mm (³⁄₁₆in) using spacers. Using the circle cutter, cut out 12 discs from each of the sugarpastes, then place on the tops of the cooled cakes.

2 Use blossom plunger cutters to cut small flowers from two shades of thinly rolled-out pink modelling paste. Then use these together with silver sugar balls of varying sizes and silver heart dragées to decorate your cupcakes.

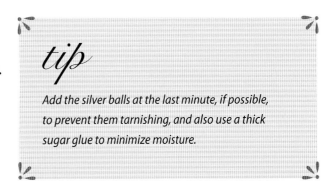

tip

Add the silver balls at the last minute, if possible, to prevent them tarnishing, and also use a thick sugar glue to minimize moisture.

Shining Stars

This is another quick and easy yet dynamic design, with an exotic Middle Eastern flavour – perfect for Christmas time and an exciting alternative to the traditional festive colour scheme.

The large cutout stars make a dramatic contrast against the blue sugarpaste background, and are gilded with edible gold lustre dust for a richly glowing effect. The finishing central jewel-like embellishment is simply created by stacking a gold and turquoise dragée with a little royal icing.

you will need ...

materials

- 24 lemon or other flavoured cupcakes, or chocolate cupcakes
- complementary flavour of syrup, alcohol, buttercream or ganache
- 650g (1lb 7oz) blue sugarpaste (rolled fondant)
- 100g (3½oz) gold modelling paste
- white vegetable fat (shortening)
- edible gold lustre dust
- sugar glue (see Sugar Recipes)
- small quantity of royal icing
- turquoise and gold dragées (sugar balls)

equipment

- non-stick work board
- large and small rolling pin
- 5mm (³⁄₁₆in) spacers
- cutters: circle cutter same diameter as top of cupcakes; 4cm (1½in) star cutter
- palette knife
- narrow spacers made from 1.5mm (¹⁄₁₆in) thick card
- waxed paper
- paintbrushes
- piping (pastry) bag with no. 1 piping tube (tip)

Making and preparing the cupcakes

1 Make and bake your chosen flavour of cupcakes (see Baking Cupcakes for recipes).

2 Brush the cakes with syrup or alcohol or add a thin layer of buttercream or ganache (see Sugar Recipes), to help keep them fresh and to help the sugarpaste stick to the cakes.

3 Knead the sugarpaste to warm, then roll out between the 5mm (³⁄₁₆in) spacers, ideally on a non-stick surface. Cut out 24 circles using a circle cutter of the appropriate size. Using a palette knife, carefully lift each paste circle onto a cupcake.

Making the star decorations

1 Roll out the gold modelling paste using the narrow spacers. Use the star cutter to cut out 24 stars. Lay on waxed paper.

2 Paint a thin layer of white vegetable fat over each star, then brush on the edible gold lustre dust. Attach a gilded star to the centre of each cupcake with sugar glue.

3 For the central decoration, fill a piping bag fitted with a no. 1 piping tube with the royal icing, then pipe a dot of icing onto the centre of the star. Top with a turquoise dragée. Pipe another dot of icing on top of the turquoise dragée and top with a gold dragée. Repeat for all the remaining stars.

Dayglo Wheelies

These zany, glow-in-the-dark cupcakes have great kids' appeal, and would go down well at a Halloween or birthday party. They are also easy enough to get the children involved in the decorating themselves, as long as they don't eat all the sweets!

All you need is a couple of different-sized circle cutters and some modelling paste in really bright, contrasting colours. The only fiddly, but fun, task is attaching the mini sprinkles around the circle edges.

you will need ...

materials

- 24 lemon or other flavoured cupcakes, or chocolate cupcakes
- complementary flavour of syrup, alcohol, buttercream or ganache
- 650g (1lb 7oz) red sugarpaste (rolled fondant)
- modelling paste: 75g (2¾oz) orange, 50g (1¾oz) black
- sugar glue (see Sugar Recipes)
- yellow sweets (candies)
- Nonpareils Sprinkles (W)

equipment

- non-stick work board
- large and small rolling pin
- 5mm (³⁄₁₆in) spacers
- circle cutters: same diameter as top of cupcakes; 2cm (¾in); 1cm (³⁄₈in)
- palette knife
- narrow spacers made from 1.5mm (¹⁄₁₆in) thick card
- paintbrush

Making and preparing the cupcakes

1 Make and bake your chosen flavour of cupcakes (see Baking Cupcakes for recipes).

2 Brush the cakes with syrup or alcohol or add a thin layer of buttercream or ganache (see Sugar Recipes), to help keep them fresh and to help the sugarpaste stick to the cakes.

3 Knead the sugarpaste to warm, then roll out between the 5mm (³⁄₁₆in) spacers, ideally on a non-stick surface. Cut out 24 circles using a circle cutter of the appropriate size. Using a palette knife, carefully lift each paste circle onto a cupcake.

Making the wheel decorations

1 Roll out the orange and black modelling pastes between the narrow spacers.

2 Using the 2cm (¾in) circle cutter, cut out 24 circles from the orange paste, then use the 1cm (³⁄₈in) circle to cut out 24 circles from the black paste. Attach an orange circle to the centre of each cupcake and then a black circle. Top with a yellow sweet using sugar glue.

3 Paint a line of sugar glue around the edge of each circle. Pick up and place Nonpareil Sprinkles (W) around the circles at even intervals using a paintbrush.

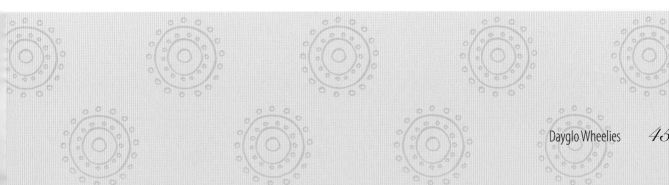

Glam Gold Hearts

These gorgeous golden little cakes would add a lovely finishing touch to the celebration table for a Golden Wedding anniversary as favours, or package them in a coordinating box tied with gold ribbon as a gift.

The heart decorations are cleverly crafted by painting an outline of sugar glue around a cutter and then attaching a length of modelling paste squeezed from a sugar shaper. The background around the hearts is then filled in with swirled and textured gold royal icing, leaving the motifs to stand out in white.

you will need ...

materials

- 24 lemon or other flavoured cupcakes, or chocolate cupcakes
- complementary flavour of syrup, alcohol, buttercream or ganache
- 650g (1lb 7oz) ivory sugarpaste (rolled fondant)
- 25g (1oz) golden brown modelling paste
- gum tragacanth
- white vegetable fat (shortening)
- sugar glue (see Sugar Recipes))
- 1 quantity of royal icing, adding 2.5ml (½ tsp) glycerine to prevent the icing setting too hard (see Sugar Recipes)
- golden brown paste colour

equipment

- non-stick work board
- large and small rolling pin
- 5mm (³⁄₁₆in) spacers
- cutters: circle cutter same diameter as top of cupcakes; small heart leaf cutter (T)
- palette knife
- sugar shaper with small round disc
- craft knife
- disposable piping (pastry) bags
- paintbrushes

Making and preparing the cupcakes

1 Make and bake your chosen flavour of cupcakes (see Baking Cupcakes for recipes).

2 Brush the cakes with syrup or alcohol or add a thin layer of buttercream or ganache (see Sugar Recipes), to help keep them fresh and to help the sugarpaste stick to the cakes.

3 Knead the sugarpaste to warm, then roll out between the 5mm (³⁄₁₆in) spacers, ideally on a non-stick surface. Cut out 24 circles using a circle cutter of the appropriate size. Using a palette knife, carefully lift each paste circle onto a cupcake.

Making the heart outlines

1 Soften the golden brown modelling paste by first kneading in some white vegetable fat to stop the paste becoming sticky and then partially dunking it into a small container of boiled water. Knead the paste again until the consistency of chewing gum. Place the softened paste with the small round disc into the sugar shaper.

2 Place the heart leaf cutter on the centre of a cupcake and then paint around it with sugar glue. Squeeze out short lengths of softened paste from a sugar shaper. Place a length along one side of the heart and cut to size with a craft knife. Take a second length and wrap it around the other side of the heart (A). Using two pieces of paste helps keep all the points sharp. Repeat for the remaining cupcakes.

A

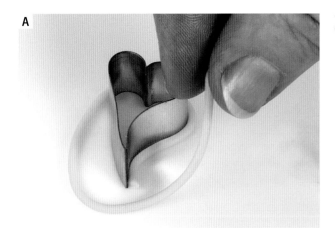

tip

If you don't have a sugar shaper, pipe the heart outlines with a no. 2 piping tube (tip) and royal icing coloured gold.

Creating the swirled gold icing

1 Colour the royal icing in a range of colours from ivory
through to gold using the golden brown paste colour (B).
Place each colour separately into a disposable piping bag, filling
the bags only half-full, and snip off the points at the very ends
of the bags.

2 Choose one of the colours and squeeze it over a small
section of the ivory sugarpaste outside the heart outline,
then change colours and repeat to create a mottled look.

3 Add texture to the icing by taking a damp paintbrush
and running it through the wet icing to add definition
and interest to the pattern (C). Neaten the edge of the icing by
removing any excess icing with a damp brush.

4 Continue one cupcake at a time, adding the icing and
texturing but leaving the hearts empty, until all the
cupcakes are complete. Leave to dry.

tip

*If your time is short, simply roll out some gold and
mid-gold modelling paste between narrow spacers,
then cut out hearts from each with the heart leaf cutter
and attach to the ivory sugarpaste-covered cupcakes.*

Time to Celebrate

The great thing about cupcakes is that they are a relatively effortless yet infinitely adaptable, creative way of celebrating the key occasions of the year or life events. What they offer is an economical and accessible alternative to the traditional-style celebration cake, ready-presented in handy individual portions with appeal to one and all. They can also be grouped together and displayed to make a high-impact centrepiece, or attractively packaged as gifts.

In this section you'll see just how varied cupcake decoration can be, like spooky characters for Halloween and beautifully crafted blooms for a Mother's Day tea party or summer engagement celebration alfresco, as well as symbolic silver horseshoes to wish someone good luck in a new venture. Yes, you can say it all with a cupcake – and in memorable style!

Springtime Hearts and Flowers

The soft, feminine colours of these pretty cupcakes, decorated with delightful daisies, stylized pink blooms and two-tone hearts, make them perfect for Mother's Day. They would also fit the bill for any other springtime celebration, such as a birthday, congratulations or welcome-home party, whether for a little girl or grown-up woman.

The flowers are simple to make using a variety of cutters, and the heart decoration is also created using cut-out heart shapes, carved down the centre in a wavy line with a craft knife.

you will need ...

materials

- 24 lemon or other flavoured cupcakes, or chocolate cupcakes
- complementary flavour of syrup, alcohol, buttercream or ganache
- sugarpaste (rolled fondant): 325g (11½oz) peachy yellow; 165g (5¾oz) each lilac and pink
- modelling paste: 50g (1¾oz) each white and pink; 25g (1oz) each deep yellow, deep pink, peachy yellow
- sugar glue (see Sugar Recipes)

equipment

- non-stick work board
- large and small rolling pin
- 5mm (³⁄₁₆in) spacers
- narrow spacers made from 1.5mm (¹⁄₁₆in) thick card
- cutters: circle cutter same diameter as top of cupcakes; 4.3cm (1⅝in) daisy cutter (FMM); 1.3cm (½in) micro-daisy cutter (LC); 2.5cm (1in) five-petal blossom cutter (FMM); small heart cutter (FMM) about 3.3cm (1¼in) high x 2.8cm (1¹⁄₁₆in) across
- palette knife
- paintbrush
- daisy centre stamps (JEM set of 6)
- cutting wheel
- craft knife

Making and preparing the cupcakes

1 Make and bake your chosen flavour of cupcakes (see Baking Cupcakes for recipes).

2 Brush the cakes with syrup or alcohol or add a thin layer of buttercream or ganache (see Sugar Recipes), to help keep them fresh and to help the sugarpaste stick to the cakes.

3 Knead each of the sugarpaste colours to warm, then roll out between the 5mm (³⁄₁₆in) spacers, ideally on a non-stick surface. Using a circle cutter of the appropriate size, cut out 12 circles from the peachy yellow sugarpaste and six each from the lilac and pink. Using a palette knife, carefully lift each paste circle onto a cupcake.

Making the large daisy design

1 Thinly roll out some white modelling paste between the narrow spacers. Place the 4.3cm (1⅝in) daisy cutter, cutter side up, on your work board or work surface, place the modelling paste over the cutter and roll over it with a small rolling pin (A).

2 Run your finger over the edges of the cutter to get a clean cut (B). Then turn the cutter over and press out the paste using a suitable paintbrush.

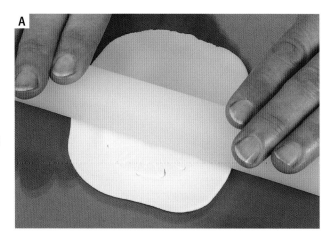

3 Cut away the petals from one side of the flower and attach them between the remaining petals (C). Attach to one of the peachy yellow cupcakes. Repeat to make another five daisies to decorate six of the peachy yellow cupcakes in total.

4 For the daisy centres, roll a ball of deep yellow modelling paste and press it into a daisy centre stamp of an appropriate size. Release the paste from the stamp, then fold one side over and pinch lightly to shape (D). Attach to the centre of one of the daisies. Repeat another five times to complete the large daisy cupcakes.

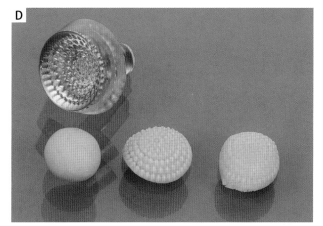

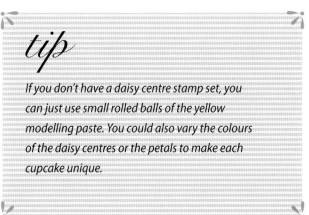

tip

If you don't have a daisy centre stamp set, you can just use small rolled balls of the yellow modelling paste. You could also vary the colours of the daisy centres or the petals to make each cupcake unique.

Making the small daisy design

1 Thinly roll out some white modelling paste between narrow spacers, then cut out 18 daisies using the micro-daisy cutter. Attach three daisies to each pink cupcake with sugar glue, spacing them apart evenly.

2 Add centres to the daisies by rolling small balls of deep yellow modelling paste and pressing them into a small daisy centre stamp of the appropriate size.

Making the pink flower design

1 To make a stem for each flower, take the cutting wheel and carefully indent a curved line from the centre to the edge of each remaining peachy yellow cupcake.

2 Thinly roll out some deep pink modelling paste between narrow spacers, then cut out six flowers using the five-petal blossom cutter. Attach one to each of the six remaining peachy yellow cupcakes with sugar glue. Roll six small balls of deep pink modelling paste and attach to the centres of the flowers.

Making the heart design

1 Thinly roll out the peachy yellow and deep pink modelling pastes between narrow spacers. Using the heart cutter, cut three hearts from each colour.

2 Use a craft knife to cut a wavy line down the centre of a pink heart. Place one cut half on top of a peachy yellow heart and cut along the edge of the wavy line. Remove the top pink half heart and attach to one of the lilac cupcakes with sugar glue, then add a cut peachy yellow half heart to form a complete heart. Repeat with the remaining hearts to decorate the other lilac cupcakes.

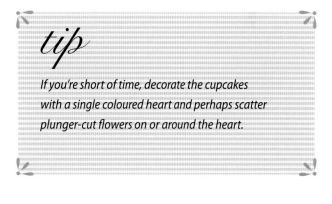

tip

If you're short of time, decorate the cupcakes with a single coloured heart and perhaps scatter plunger-cut flowers on or around the heart.

Fall Fairies

These are fairy cakes with a difference! Cupcakes are adorned with a fantastical 3D fairy and highly realistic-looking oak leaves and acorn cups – lovely for celebrating Halloween or a little girl's autumn birthday.

This is a great opportunity to put your painting skills to work in bringing the enchanting fairy figures, formed using a commercial mould, to life. The leaves are made with a cutter and veiner, and left to dry on an undulated surface to produce their convincing curled shape.

you will need ...

materials

- 24 lemon or other flavoured cupcakes, or chocolate cupcakes
- complementary flavour of syrup, alcohol, buttercream or ganache
- 650g (1lb 7oz) purple sugarpaste (rolled fondant)
- modelling paste: 75g (2¾ oz) flesh, 100g (3½oz) golden brown
- paste colours and dust colours of your choice, for painting fairies
- clear spirit, such as gin or vodka
- sugar glue (see Sugar Recipes)

equipment

- non-stick work board
- large and small rolling pin
- 5mm (³⁄₁₆in) spacers
- cutters: circle cutter same diameter as top of cupcakes; oak leaf cutter, 2.3cm (1⁵⁄₁₆in)
- moulds: small fairy; acorn cup (DP)
- palette knife
- paint palette
- paintbrushes
- narrow spacers made from 1.5mm (¹⁄₁₆in) thick card
- leaf veiner
- undulated foam
- ball tool

Making and preparing the cupcakes

1 Make and bake your chosen flavour of cupcakes (see Baking Cupcakes for recipes).

2 Brush the cakes with syrup or alcohol or add a thin layer of buttercream or ganache (see Sugar Recipes), to help keep them fresh and to help the sugarpaste stick to the cakes.

3 Knead the sugarpaste to warm, then roll out between the 5mm (³⁄₁₆in) spacers, ideally on a non-stick surface. Cut out 24 circles using a circle cutter of the appropriate size. Using a palette knife, carefully lift each paste circle onto a cupcake.

Making and painting the fairies

1 Knead a small amount of the flesh modelling paste to warm it, then roll a sausage of paste slightly larger than the mould cavity. Insert the paste into the mould, ensuring that the sugar surface being placed in the mould is perfectly smooth – if there are small joins visible, they will probably also be noticeable on your finished piece!

2 Push the paste into the mould firmly to make sure that the deeper sections of the mould are filled. Then stroke the paste around the edges of the mould with your finger to help it fill the mould completely.

3 Remove the excess paste with a palette knife so that the back of the mould is flat. To remove the paste, carefully flex the mould to release. Repeat the process to make a total of 24 fairy figures.

4 To paint the fairies, dilute suitable paste and dust colours separately with clear spirit in a paint palette and apply with paintbrushes (see Painting Techniques). Leave to dry.

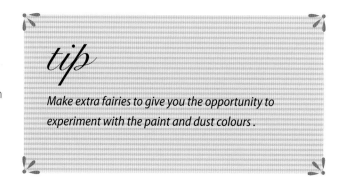

tip

Make extra fairies to give you the opportunity to experiment with the paint and dust colours .

Creating the oak leaves and acorn cups

1 Roll out the golden brown flower paste between the narrow spacers and use the oak leaf cutter to cut out 24 leaves. Place each leaf in the double-sided veiner and press together to vein. Place on undulated foam and leave to dry.

2 Place a pea-sized ball of golden brown flower paste in the acorn cup mould. Press the paste into the mould with the larger end of the ball tool and circle the tool so that the paste spreads up to the top of the mould (A). Remove and repeat to make a total of 24 or more cups (you may like to add a couple of cups to some of the cupcakes). Leave to dry.

To finish

Secure an oak leaf and one or two acorn cups to each cupcake with sugar glue, then add a fairy.

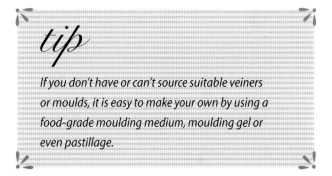

tip

If you don't have or can't source suitable veiners or moulds, it is easy to make your own by using a food-grade moulding medium, moulding gel or even pastillage.

Spooky Characters

Children will love these 'scary' cupcakes, topped with jet black sugarpaste and decorated with classic ghoulish Halloween images. They really will set just the right thrilling, 'chilling' atmosphere for the event.

These designs are ultra easy to create using a set of Halloween-themed cutters, with the wicked cut-out motifs eye-poppingly contrasted against the black sugarpaste background. Large, bright star sprinkles add a fun finishing decorative element.

you will need …

materials

- 24 lemon or other flavoured cupcakes, or chocolate cupcakes
- complementary flavour of syrup, alcohol, buttercream or ganache
- 650g (1lb 7oz) black sugarpaste (rolled fondant)
- modelling paste: 50g (1¾oz) each white and orange
- sugar glue (see Sugar Recipes)
- Star Sprinkles (W)

equipment

- non-stick work board
- large and small rolling pin
- 5mm (³⁄₁₆in) spacers
- cutters: circles – same diameter as top of cupcakes; Halloween cutters (PC Halloween set or FMM Special Occasion Tappits)
- palette knife
- narrow spacers made from 1.5mm (¹⁄₁₆in) thick card

Making and preparing the cupcakes

1 Make and bake your chosen flavour of cupcakes (see Baking Cupcakes for recipes).

2 Brush the cakes with syrup or alcohol or add a thin layer of buttercream or ganache (see Sugar Recipes), to help keep them fresh and to help the sugarpaste stick to the cakes.

3 Knead the sugarpaste to warm, then roll out between the 5mm (³⁄₁₆in) spacers, ideally on a non-stick surface. Cut out 24 circles using a circle cutter of the appropriate size. Using a palette knife, carefully lift each paste circle onto a cupcake.

Making the Halloween decorations

1 Roll out the white and orange modelling pastes thinly between the narrow spacers. Using the Halloween cutters, cut out 12 ghosts from the white paste and 12 jack o'lanterns from the orange paste. If using Tappit cutters, place your thinly rolled-out modelling paste over the top of the cutter, roll over the paste with a rolling pin, then run a finger around the top of the cutter to achieve a nice clean cut. Finally, tap the cutter firmly on your work surface to release the paste shape. Attach one Halloween character to each cupcake with sugar glue.

2 Decorate the ghost cupcakes with Star Sprinkles.

Bewitching Bats

These dramatic bat-adorned cupcakes with their deep blue night-sky backgrounds are just the thing for a kids' Halloween party – great for making a centrepiece display so that they seem to be swooping menacingly over the table, or for popping into party bags as a spooky treat.

The children can also have lots of fun helping to create the simple decorations, using a cutter from a Halloween set and scattering over edible sparkle dust and colourful star sprinkles to add that extra touch of magic.

you will need ...

materials

- 24 lemon or other flavoured cupcakes, or chocolate cupcakes
- complementary flavour of syrup, alcohol, buttercream or ganache
- 650g (1lb 7oz) navy sugarpaste (rolled fondant)
- blue edible sparkle dust
- 50g (1¾oz) black modelling paste
- sugar glue (see Sugar Recipes)
- Star Sprinkles (W)

equipment

- non-stick work board
- large and small rolling pin
- 5mm (³⁄₁₆in) spacers
- cutters: circle cutter same diameter as top of cupcakes; bat cutters (PC Halloween set or FMM Special Occasion Tappits)
- palette knife
- narrow cutters made from 1.5mm (¹⁄₁₆in) thick card

Making and preparing the cupcakes

1 Make and bake your chosen flavour of cupcakes (see Baking Cupcakes for recipes).

2 Brush the cakes with syrup or alcohol or add a thin layer of buttercream or ganache (see Sugar Recipes), to help keep them fresh and to help the sugarpaste stick to the cakes.

3 Knead the sugarpaste to warm, then roll out between the 5mm (³⁄₁₆in) spacers, ideally on a non-stick surface. Cut out 24 circles using a circle cutter of the appropriate size. Using a palette knife, carefully lift each paste circle onto a cupcake. Dust each paste circle with blue edible sparkle dust.

Making the bat and star decorations

1 Roll out the black modelling paste between the narrow spacers. Cut out 24 bats using the bat cutter. If using a Tappit cutter, place your thinly rolled-out modelling paste over the top of the cutter, roll over the paste with a rolling pin, then run a finger around the top of the cutter to achieve a nice clean cut. Finally, tap the cutter firmly on your work surface to release the paste shape.

2 Attach a bat to the centre of each cupcake with sugar glue, then dot a few Star Sprinkles around each bat.

Silken Rosebuds

Roses are the ultimate symbol of romantic love and therefore guaranteed to work well for any engagement, wedding or anniversary celebration. And these are especially sumptuous and sophisticated, fashioned to resemble fabric flowers and combined with opulent fabric-effect swirls and loops.

The rosebuds are simply made from folded and rolled-up strips of modelling paste, while the faux fabric drapes and ribbons are created by gathering and shaping thinly rolled-out pieces or strips of modelling paste.

you will need ...

materials

- 24 lemon or other flavoured cupcakes, or chocolate cupcakes
- complementary flavour of syrup, alcohol, buttercream or ganache
- 650g (1lb 7oz) white sugarpaste (rolled fondant)
- modelling paste: 250g (9oz) each deep pink, light pink, mid-pink; 100g (3½oz) lilac, 50g (1¾oz) purple
- sugar glue (see Sugar Recipes))
- 8–10mm (⁵⁄₁₅–⅜in) silver dragées (sugar balls)

equipment

- non-stick work board
- large and small rolling pin
- 5mm (³⁄₁₆in) spacers
- circle cutter same diameter as top of cupcakes
- palette knife
- narrow spacers made from 1.5mm (¹⁄₁₆in) thick card
- scissors
- cutting wheel

Making and preparing the cupcakes

1 Make and bake your chosen flavour of cupcakes (see Baking Cupcakes for recipes).

2 Brush the cakes with syrup or alcohol or add a thin layer of buttercream or ganache (see Sugar Recipes), to help keep them fresh and to help the sugarpaste stick to the cakes.

3 Knead the sugarpaste to warm, then roll out between the 5mm (³⁄₁₆in) spacers, ideally on a non-stick surface. Cut out 24 circles using a circle cutter of the appropriate size. Using a palette knife, carefully lift each paste circle onto a cupcake.

Making the faux fabric rosebuds

1 Roll out the deep pink modelling paste between the narrow spacers. Fold over a section of the paste and cut the fold to a width of 1.5cm (⅝in) and length of 13cm (5in). Starting at one end of the folded paste, roll up the paste to form a spiral, pressing the cut edge together and gathering it slightly as you roll to create fullness and space in the flower (A).

tip

It's often easier to roll the modelling paste into a sausage the correct length and then roll it flat with a rolling pin.

2 Neaten the back of the rose by cutting off the excess paste with scissors (B). Make 24 of these rosebuds in total.

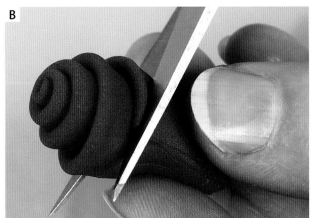

Making the fabric-effect decorations

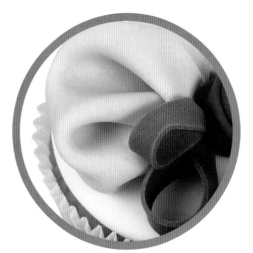

1   Roll out the other modelling paste colours between the narrow spacers. Cut the paste into rough rectangular or square shapes of different sizes. Pick up either two or four corners and bring them to the centre, then arrange a selection of the gathered and draped paste on each of the cupcakes.

2   To make ribbon strips, cut a freehand curvy shape using a cutting wheel and arrange on some of the cakes.

3   To make ribbon loops, cut narrow strips of the rolled-out modelling paste, then pinch the ends of each strip together to form loops. Place on their sides to partially dry before adding to some of the cupcakes.

The finishing touch

Attach a small or large rosebud to each cupcake, then add a few silver dragées to complete the decoration.

Hearts Entwined

Hearts are another enduring symbol of love, and these hold special significance in being linked together in a couple. Their scrolled design looks particularly decorative against the classic deep red backdrop.

To achieve these outlined shapes, they are first indented onto the sugarpaste with a cutter, then painted with sugar glue and topped with lines of modelling paste squeezed from a sugar shaper. The lines are then gilded with gold dust to enrich them.

you will need ...

materials

- 24 lemon or other flavoured cupcakes, or chocolate cupcakes
- complementary flavour of syrup, alcohol, buttercream or ganache
- 650g (1lb 7oz) red sugarpaste (rolled fondant)
- sugar glue (see Sugar Recipes)
- 50g (1¾oz) golden brown modelling paste
- white vegetable fat (shortening)
- confectioners' glaze
- gold edible dust
- gold dragées (sugar balls)

equipment

- non-stick work board
- large and small rolling pin
- 5mm (³⁄₁₆in) spacers
- cutters: circle cutter same diameter as top of cupcakes; small heart cutter
- palette knife
- fine paintbrush
- sugar shaper with small round disc
- craft knife

Making and preparing the cupcakes

1 Make and bake your chosen flavour of cupcakes (see Baking Cupcakes for recipes).

2 Brush the cakes with syrup or alcohol or add a thin layer of buttercream or ganache (see Sugar Recipes), to help keep them fresh and to help the sugarpaste stick to the cakes.

3 Knead the sugarpaste to warm, then roll out between the 5mm (³⁄₁₆in) spacers, ideally on a non-stick surface. Cut out 24 circles using a circle cutter of the appropriate size. Using a palette knife, carefully lift each paste circle onto a cupcake.

Making the scrolled hearts decoration

1 Use the heart cutter to indent a heart in the centre of each cupcake. Holding the cutter at a slight angle, indent the second heart behind the first, taking care not to indent lines within the first.

2 Dip a fine paintbrush into sugar glue and paint around the outlines of the joined indented hearts, adding the scrolls as shown in the photo detail on the right.

3 Soften the modelling paste by adding a little white vegetable fat, to stop it sticking, and boiled water to soften it. Place the softened paste in the sugar shaper with the small round disc and squeeze out a length.

4 Place the length of modelling paste over the outline of glue-painted hearts and adjust its shape with a finger and/or paintbrush (A). Cut the paste where necessary with a craft knife.

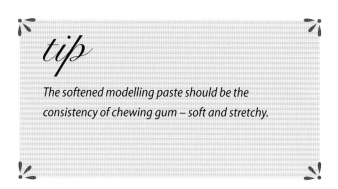

tip

The softened modelling paste should be the consistency of chewing gum – soft and stretchy.

A

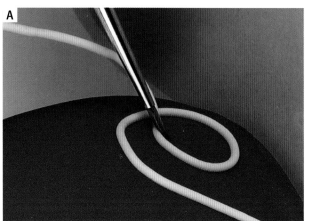

The finishing touches

1 Gild the hearts by mixing edible gold dust with some confectioners' glaze and, using a fine paintbrush, paint over the heart shapes (B).

2 To add the gold dragées, dip a paintbrush in sugar glue and paint a dot either side of the hearts. Place a gold dragée over each glue dot and press it fractionally into the surface of the sugarpaste to secure.

B

tip

Apply the same principle to decorate your cupcakes with other shapes of cutter to create interesting patterns.

Celebrated Scholar

These characterful bright and bold cupcakes are perfect for marking the special occasion of a graduation or congratulating someone on passing their exams with flying colours in a fun, memorable way.

The deep blue sugarpaste really makes the motifs stand out and achieve maximum impact, and they are further enhanced by being painted with diluted paste colours to highlight their details and add visual interest.

you will need ...

materials

- 24 lemon or other flavoured cupcakes, or chocolate cupcakes
- complementary flavour of syrup, alcohol, buttercream or ganache
- 650g (1lb 7oz) blue sugarpaste (rolled fondant)
- modelling paste: 50g (13/4oz) each yellow and cream; 25g (1oz) red
- paste colours: selection of browns, red and orange
- clear spirit, such as gin or vodka
- sugar glue (see Sugar Recipes)

equipment

- non-stick work board
- large and small rolling pin
- 5mm (3/16in) spacers
- narrow spacers made from 1.5mm (1/16in) thick card
- cutters: circles – same diameter as top of cupcakes;
- open book and sun cutters (FMM Special Occasion Tappits)
- palette knife
- craft knife
- paint palette
- paintbrushes

Making and preparing the cupcakes

1 Make and bake your chosen flavour of cupcakes (see Baking Cupcakes for recipes).

2 Brush the cakes with syrup or alcohol or add a thin layer of buttercream or ganache (see Sugar Recipes), to help keep them fresh and to help the sugarpaste stick to the cakes.

3 Knead the sugarpaste to warm, then roll out between the 5mm (3/16in) spacers, ideally on a non-stick surface. Cut out 24 circles using a circle cutter of the appropriate size. Using a palette knife, carefully lift each paste circle onto a cupcake.

Making the sun and book

1 Thinly roll out the yellow modelling paste. Place the paste over the top of the sun Tappit cutter, roll over the paste with a rolling pin, then run a finger around the top of the cutter to achieve a nice clean cut. Finally, tap the cutter firmly on your work surface to release the shape. Cut 24 suns.

2 Thinly roll out the red and cream modelling pastes and cut out 24 books from each using the book cutter, as described in step 1. Using a craft knife, separate the bookmark from the book pages and assemble on the cupcakes so that the pages are cream and the bookmark red. Attach a sun to each book.

3 Separately dilute the paste colours with clear spirit. Using paintbrushes, apply a colourwash over the book pages to give a parchment look. Paint over the sun with yellow, adding a touch of orange to the rays. Paint over the bookmark with red.

Lucky Charms

There is no mistaking the good luck message that's conveyed by a horseshoe, and this cupcake design is applicable to a whole range of occasions where that sentiment is appropriate, from a new job or home to a travel expedition or even a wedding.

The horseshoes are simply cut out from grey modelling paste using a cutter and then given a metallic-effect treatment by brushing with white vegetable fat and dusting with edible silver dust. They make an especially dramatic display set against navy sugarpaste.

you will need ...

materials

- 24 lemon or other flavoured cupcakes, or chocolate cupcakes
- complementary flavour of syrup, alcohol, buttercream or ganache
- 650g (1lb 7oz) navy sugarpaste (rolled fondant)
- 50g (13/4oz) grey modelling paste
- white vegetable fat (shortening)
- edible silver lustre dust
- Star Sprinkles (W)
- sugar glue (see Sugar Recipes)

equipment

- non-stick work board
- large and small rolling pin
- 5mm (3/16in) spacers
- cutters: circles – same diameter as top of cupcakes; horseshoe cutter (FMM Celebration Tappits)
- palette knife
- narrow spacers made from 1.5mm (1/16in) thick card
- paintbrush and soft dusting brush

Making and preparing the cupcakes

1 Make and bake your chosen flavour of cupcakes (see Baking Cupcakes for recipes).

2 Brush the cakes with syrup or alcohol or add a thin layer of buttercream or ganache (see Sugar Recipes), to help keep them fresh and to help the sugarpaste stick to the cakes.

3 Knead the sugarpaste to warm, then roll out between the 5mm (3/16in) spacers, ideally on a non-stick surface. Cut out 24 circles using a circle cutter of the appropriate size. Using a palette knife, carefully lift each paste circle onto a cupcake.

Making the horseshoe decoration

1 Roll out the grey modelling paste between the narrow spacers. Place the paste over the top of the Tappit cutter, roll over the paste with a rolling pin, then run a finger around the top of the cutter to achieve a nice clean cut. Finally, tap the cutter firmly on your work surface to release the paste shape. Cut out 24 horseshoes.

2 Brush over each horseshoe with white vegetable fat, then dust with edible silver lustre dust. Attach a horseshoe to the centre of each cupcake with sugar glue and surround with some Star Sprinkles.

Daisy Delights

Daisies with their bright cheery faces are sure to make everyone break out in smiles, and they encapsulate the essence of a fresh, sunny day. So these cupcakes are the perfect choice for any late spring or early summer celebration, whether alfresco or indoors.

These wonderfully flamboyant blooms are made by cutting out and layering two flowers using a daisy cutter, to make them extra generous, and the petal tips are then curled with a ball tool to give them a naturalistic look. The centre is created using a mould, and is framed by a fringed strip of modelling paste.

you will need . . .

materials

- 24 lemon or other flavoured cupcakes, or chocolate cupcakes
- complementary flavour of syrup, alcohol, buttercream or ganache
- 650g (1lb 7oz) light cream sugarpaste (rolled fondant)
- modelling pastes: 100g (31/2oz) orange, 25g (1oz) yellow
- edible orange dust
- sugar glue (see Sugar Recipes)

equipment

- non-stick work board
- large and small rolling pin
- 5mm (³⁄₁₆in) spacers
- cutters: circle cutter same diameter as top of cupcakes; daisy cutters (FMM daisy collection; PME daisy marguerite)
- palette knife
- narrow spacers made from 1.5mm (¹⁄₁₆in) thick card
- paintbrush and soft dusting brush
- foam pad
- ball tool
- cutting wheel
- daisy centre moulds (JEM) (optional)

Making and preparing the cupcakes

1 Make and bake your chosen flavour of cupcakes (see Baking Cupcakes for recipes).

2 Brush the cakes with syrup or alcohol or add a thin layer of buttercream or ganache (see Sugar Recipes), to help keep them fresh and to help the sugarpaste stick to the cakes.

3 Knead the sugarpaste to warm, then roll out between the 5mm (³⁄₁₆in) spacers, ideally on a non-stick surface. Cut out 24 circles using a circle cutter of the appropriate size. Using a palette knife, carefully lift each paste circle onto a cupcake.

Making the daisy decorations

1 Roll out the orange modelling paste between the narrow spacers. Select a daisy cutter from the set – choose whichever size you like that will fit within the sugarpaste disc. Place the cutter, cutter side up, on your work board, place the modelling paste over the cutter and roll over it with a small rolling pin. Run your finger over the edges of the cutter to obtain a clean cut (A), then turn the cutter over and carefully press out the paste using a paintbrush.

tip

Thoroughly knead the modelling paste to warm it before rolling it out thinly.

A

2 Place the modelling paste daisy on a foam pad, or the palm of your hand, and run the small end of a ball tool from the tip of a petal towards the centre (B) to curl the ends.

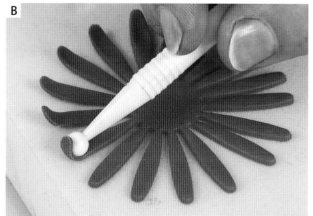

3 Cut a second daisy, curl the ends of the petals as before and place on top of the first.

4 Thinly roll out a strip of orange paste and cut into the edge repeatedly with a cutting wheel to fringe (C). Cut the fringe into a narrow strip, cutting close but not into the fringing itself. Place the fringed strip around the edge of the flower centre.

5 Roll a ball of yellow modelling paste and press it into the daisy centre mould before attaching it to the flower. Finally, use a soft dusting brush to dust the very centre of the flower with edible orange dust.

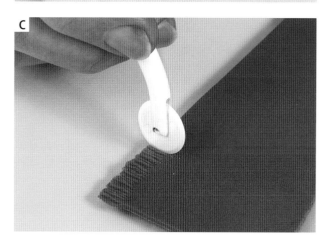

6 Repeat the above steps to make 24 daisies in total, using different sizes of cutter to vary the size of the flowers, then attach one to the centre of each cupcake with sugar glue.

Poppy Crops

No wonder the poppy is such a popular flower, with its delicate,
fluttery petals of vivid red suddenly turning to velvet black at their
base, and this design successfully captures its unique qualities in
modelling paste. These cupcakes would play a memorable role
at a Mother's Day tea party or special birthday celebration.

Despite their arty look, the poppy blooms are straightforward to create
using an embosser-cum-cutter. You can achieve a really striking effect
by varying the positioning and trimming of the poppy on each cupcake
and then grouping them together to form a stunning centrepiece.

you will need ...

materials

- 24 lemon or other flavoured cupcakes, or chocolate cupcakes
- complementary flavour of syrup, alcohol, buttercream or ganache
- 650g (1lb 7oz) ivory sugarpaste (rolled fondant)
- modelling pastes: 200g (7oz) red, 25g (1oz) black, 35g (1¼oz) green
- sugar glue (see Sugar Recipes)

equipment

- non-stick work board
- large and small rolling pin
- 5mm (³⁄₁₆in) spacers
- circle cutter same diameter as top of cupcakes
- palette knife
- narrow spacers made from 1.5mm (¹⁄₁₆in) thick card
- poppy embosser/cutter (PC)
- craft knife

Making and preparing the cupcakes

1 Make and bake your chosen flavour of cupcakes (see Baking Cupcakes for recipes).

2 Brush the cakes with syrup or alcohol or add a thin layer of buttercream or ganache (see Sugar Recipes), to help keep them fresh and to help the sugarpaste stick to the cakes.

3 Knead the sugarpaste to warm, then roll out between the 5mm (³⁄₁₆in) spacers, ideally on a non-stick surface. Cut out 24 circles using a circle cutter of the appropriate size. Using a palette knife, carefully lift each paste circle onto a cupcake.

Making the poppy decorations

1 Roll out the red, black and green modelling pastes between the narrow spacers. Using the poppy embosser/cutter, emboss the poppy onto the red paste, the base of the petals onto the black and the poppy centre onto the green. Use a craft knife held vertically to cut along the embossed lines to separate the sections.

2 Emboss and cut out 24 poppies in total. Using sugar glue, attach the appropriate sections of the cut out poppies to each cupcake slightly off-centre, then trim the edge to fit.

Baby Toy Joys

This cute collection of cupcakes would make the ideal addition to a baby shower or christening celebration, or package them up prettily as a gift for the proud parents of a new arrival to the family.

Nursery cutters make easy work of creating these delightful designs, cut from modelling paste in soft, pastel-coloured shades in keeping with the baby theme. Some of the designs are further embellished with dainty flowers made using a set of mini blossom cutters, with little rolled balls of modelling paste added for the flower centres.

you will need …

materials

- 24 lemon or other flavoured cupcakes, or chocolate cupcakes
- complementary flavour of syrup, alcohol, buttercream or ganache
- 650g (1lb 7oz) pale pink sugarpaste (rolled fondant)
- sugar glue (see Sugar Recipes)
- modelling pastes: 100g (3½oz) white, 25g (1oz) each pink, mint green, golden brown, lilac

equipment

- non-stick work board
- large and small rolling pin
- 5mm (³⁄₁₆in) spacers
- cutters: circles – same diameter as top of cupcakes and smaller; nursery cutters (PC Make a Cradle set and Nursery Set and Toy Tappits by FMM); small heart cutter; set of blossom plunger cutters (PME)
- palette knife
- narrow spacers made from 1.5mm (¹⁄₁₆in) thick card
- paintbrush

Making and preparing the cupcakes

1 Make and bake your chosen flavour of cupcakes (see Baking Cupcakes for recipes).

2 Brush the cakes with syrup or alcohol or add a thin layer of buttercream or ganache (see Sugar Recipes), to help keep them fresh and to help the sugarpaste stick to the cakes.

3 Knead the sugarpaste to warm, then roll out between the 5mm (³⁄₁₆in) spacers, ideally on a non-stick surface. Cut out 24 circles using a circle cutter of the appropriate size. Using a palette knife, carefully lift each paste circle onto a cupcake.

4 Thinly roll out the white modelling paste, ideally between narrow spacers, and cut out 24 smaller circles. Place one in the centre of each cupcake.

Making the toy decorations

1 Roll out the pink modelling paste between the narrow spacers. Place the paste over the top of the rabbit Tappit cutter, roll over the paste with a rolling pin, then run a finger around the top of the cutter to achieve a nice clean cut. Finally, tap the cutter firmly on your work surface to release the paste shape. Cut out six rabbits, then attach one to six of the cupcakes, on the left-hand side of the white sugarpaste discs.

2 Using the nursery cutters, cut out six rocking horses and six teddies from the thinly rolled-out mint green and golden brown modelling pastes. Attach a rocking horse to six of the cupcakes, positioning it to align with the edge of the white disc. Add a teddy bear to another six cupcakes, slightly off-centre.

3 Cut six small hearts from thinly rolled-out pink modelling paste. Pinch the end of each heart to a fine point and attach one to the side of each bear.

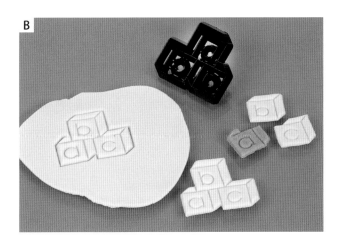

4 For the alphabet brick design, cut out six sets of bricks each from the thinly rolled-out lilac, golden brown and pink modelling pastes. Separate the bricks with a craft knife, then attach to the remaining six cupcakes using one brick of each colour per group (B).

5 Use a blossom plunger cutter to cut 18 small blossoms from the lilac modelling paste. Add a centre to each flower by rolling and attaching a small ball of golden brown modelling paste. Attach a group of three flowers next to each rabbit (C).

6 Cut 18 tiny lilac flowers with a blossom plunger cutter and add flower centres, as in Step 3, then attach a row of three to each rocker of the rocking horses.

Animal Magic

Animals have such a powerful, universal appeal and never fail to intrigue and entertain us, so they make a great subject and source of inspiration for cake designs. And using them to adorn a set of cupcakes gives you the opportunity to create a whole group of creature characters or wildlife scenes.

These fun projects offer lots of scope for painting, to recreate the fabulous colours and markings of the real-life creatures, in addition to using commercial moulds or modelling your own to form their shapes. But as with we humans, animals are not always perfectly formed and symmetrical, so you don't have to worry unduly if your decorations are a little lopsided – it will only add to their personality and charm! And if you prefer, you can always dispense with reality and dream up your own imaginary colour schemes and patterns.

Party Pigs

Anyone can see that these are definitely party-going pigs, looking
up expectantly and smiling. There's an interesting mix of piggy
characters or 'breeds' here, with their varying skin colours.

The pigs' heads are ingeniously formed from balls of modelling paste,
the smiley mouth indented with a piping tube and the nostrils with the
end of a paintbrush. The earth-like cupcake tops are made by pressing
a pan scourer into the soft sugarpaste to add an all-over texture.

you will need ...

materials

- 24 lemon or other flavoured cupcakes, or chocolate cupcakes
- complementary flavour of syrup, alcohol, buttercream or ganache
- 650g (1lb 7oz) brown sugarpaste (rolled fondant)
- modelling paste: 240g (8¾oz) flesh, 120g (4¼oz) each golden brown and black
- sugar glue (see Sugar Recipes)

equipment

- non-stick work board
- large and small rolling pin
- 5mm (³⁄₁₆in) spacers
- circle cutter same diameter as top of cupcakes
- palette knife
- pan scourer
- no. 4 piping tube (tip) (PME)
- Dresden tool
- paintbrush
- cocktail stick (toothpick)
- scissors

Making and preparing the cupcakes

1 Make and bake your chosen flavour of cupcakes (see Baking Cupcakes for recipes).

2 Brush the cakes with syrup or alcohol or add a thin layer of buttercream or ganache (see Sugar Recipes), to help keep them fresh and to help the sugarpaste stick to the cakes.

3 Knead the sugarpaste to warm, then roll out between the 5mm (³⁄₁₆in) spacers, ideally on a non-stick surface. Take a pan scourer and firmly press it into the soft sugarpaste to add texture (A). Cut out 24 circles using a circle cutter of the appropriate size. Using a palette knife, carefully lift each paste circle onto a cupcake.

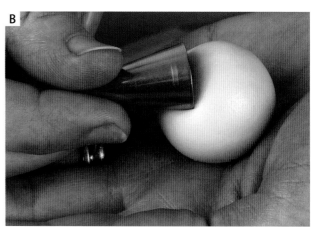

Making the pigs' heads

1 Take 15g (½oz) of one colour of modelling paste and roll it into a 3cm (1⅛in) ball. Take the no. 4 piping tube and, using the larger end, indent a mouth by holding the tube at an angle to one ball half (B). Indent the corners of the mouth using the smaller end of the tube, again holding it at an angle to the face. Next, open up the smile by using the wider end of the Dresden tool.

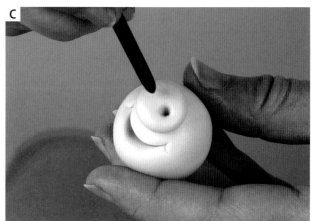

2 For the snout, roll a 1.3cm (½in) ball of modelling paste, flatten it slightly and attach it to the front of the face with sugar glue. Take a paintbrush and insert the end twice into the snout to form nostrils (C).

3   For the eyes, use a cocktail stick to indent two eyes above the snout. Then roll two small balls of black modelling paste and glue them in place with sugar glue.

4   Cut the curved surface away at the back of the head with scissors. Glue the pig's head onto the centre of a cupcake with sugar glue. For the ears, roll two pea-sized balls of paste. Pinch one end of each to flatten and widen it, then pinch the other to a point. Attach the wider end of each ear in position on the top of the pig's head using sugar glue (D).

5   Create a further 23 pigs' heads, one for each of the remaining cupcakes, using a variety of modelling pastes. Cut out spots freehand from black modelling paste and attach to some of the flesh-coloured pigs' heads.

tip

To give the pigs a beady-eyed look, glaze the eyeballs using confectioners' glaze applied with a fine paintbrush.

Fluttering Butterflies

These beautiful, delicate butterflies look amazingly lifelike, seeming to hover over the deep blue sugarpaste, which serves as a good complementary background to the oranges and warm brown tones of their wings. The cupcakes would make a special gift for an insect lover.

If painting is your forte, then this is the ideal project for you. Once the butterflies have been formed using the commercial mould and the antennae inserted, you can become fully absorbed in recreating the intricate markings of real butterflies using diluted paste colours.

you will need . . .

materials

- pastillage
- 48 black stamens for the antennae
- sugar glue (see Sugar Recipes)
- paste colours: yellow, orange, black, brown, cream
- clear spirit, such as gin or vodka
- 24 lemon or other flavoured cupcakes, or chocolate cupcakes
- complementary flavour of syrup, alcohol, buttercream or ganache
- 650g (1lb 7oz) deep blue sugarpaste (rolled fondant)

equipment

- non-stick work board
- large and small rolling pin
- small butterfly cutter; circle cutter same diameter as top of cupcakes
- small butterfly mould or veiner (optional)
- glass-headed dressmakers' pin
- 'V'-shaped card former
- paint palette
- paintbrushes
- 5mm (³⁄₁₆in) spacers
- palette knife

Making the butterflies

1 Thinly roll out some pastillage and cut out 24 small butterflies using the cutter. Add a small sausage of paste for a body. If desired, vein the wings in a mould or veiner.

2 Use a pin to make a hole either side of each butterfly head. Cut the antennae to length, dip the ends in sugar glue and insert into the holes. Leave to dry on a 'V'-shaped card former.

3 Using a paint palette, separately dilute each paste colour with clear spirit. Paint the butterflies to resemble real butterflies. Apply the base colours first and leave to dry before adding the more detailed markings with a fine paintbrush.

Making and finishing the cupcakes

1 Make and bake your chosen flavour of cupcakes (see Baking Cupcakes for recipes).

2 Brush the cakes with syrup or alcohol or add a thin layer of buttercream or ganache (see Sugar Recipes), to help keep them fresh and to help the sugarpaste stick to the cakes.

3 Knead the sugarpaste to warm, then roll out between the 5mm (³⁄₁₆in) spacers, ideally on a non-stick surface. Cut out 24 circles using a circle cutter of the appropriate size. Using a palette knife, carefully lift each paste circle onto a cupcake. Attach a butterfly to each cupcake with sugar glue.

Fleecy Flock

Why not invite this flock of adorable sheep, with their gorgeous golden-curled fleeces set against a blue-sky backdrop, to an outdoor summer celebration for a taste of the rural idyll.

This is an opportunity to practise your piping skills to achieve even swirls and dots of buttercream, although if you are short of time (or a steady hand!) you could just pipe haphazard wiggly lines for the fleece instead. The wrinkly legs are easy and fun to pipe, and the sheep's heads are also piped but then smoothed with a hot brush.

you will need ...

materials

- 24 lemon or other flavoured cupcakes, or chocolate cupcakes
- complementary flavour of syrup, alcohol, buttercream or ganache
- 650g (1lb 7oz) purple-blue sugarpaste (rolled fondant)
- 1 quantity of buttercream (see Sugar Recipes)
- paste colours: golden brown (Spectral – Autumn Leaf), dark brown
- sugar glue (see Sugar Recipes)

equipment

- non-stick work board
- large and small rolling pin
- 5mm (³⁄₁₆in) spacers
- circle cutter same diameter as top of cupcakes
- palette knife
- reusable piping (pastry) bag and coupler
- piping tubes (tip): nos. 4, 2
- soft, flat-headed paintbrush

Making and preparing the cupcakes

1 Make and bake your chosen flavour of cupcakes (see Baking Cupcakes for recipes).

2 Brush the cakes with syrup or alcohol or add a thin layer of buttercream or ganache (see Sugar Recipes), to help keep them fresh and to help the sugarpaste stick to the cakes.

3 Knead the sugarpaste to warm, then roll out between the 5mm (³⁄₁₆in) spacers, ideally on a non-stick surface. Cut out 24 circles using a circle cutter of the appropriate size. Using a palette knife, carefully lift each paste circle onto a cupcake.

Piping the sheep decorations

1 Using a reusable piping bag and coupler fitted with a no. 4 piping tube, pipe on swirls and dots in the centre of the sugarpaste discs to create the sheep's fleecy bodies (A).

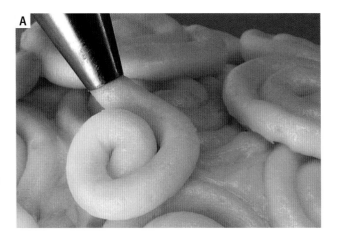

2 Colour all but a small amount of the remaining buttercream with golden brown paste colour to a rich shade of golden brown. Have a saucepan of simmering water nearby and a soft, flat-headed paintbrush. Again using the no. 4 tube, pipe the sheep's heads in the centre of the bodies. Dip the paintbrush into the hot water to heat it, which prevents the icing sticking to the brush, then remove the excess water. Smooth the heads by making long, smooth strokes down them with the hot brush.

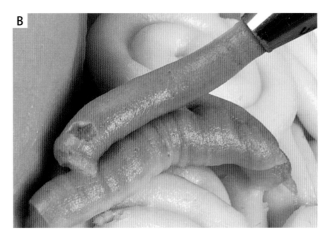

3 Darken the golden brown buttercream you have left over with a little more of the golden brown colour to make a richer brown. To pipe the ears, using a no. 2 piping tube and starting at a sheep's head, pipe two lines to form the curved shape of the ear, then add a line on top of the first two (B). Use the heated paintbrush to smooth the buttercream to shape it, as in Step 2. Repeat for the other ear and then for all the remaining sheep's heads.

4 For the sheep's legs, still using the same buttercream and piping tube, place the piping tube a fraction away from a sheep's body and squeeze the piping bag until the buttercream squeezed out is twice the diameter of the tube. Move the tube a fraction away from the body and squeeze again. Continue moving and squeezing in the same way to achieve a wrinkled/textured line of icing (C). Repeat for the other leg and for all the remaining sheep.

5 For the sheep's eyes, using a small amount of the remaining uncoloured buttercream and the no. 4 tube, pipe two dots onto each sheep's head. Colour the remaining buttercream dark brown with the dark brown paste colour and use the no. 2 piping tube to pipe pupils onto the lower half of each eye.

6 For the sheep's noses, use the no. 2 tube and the dark brown buttercream to pipe a wide heart shape at the lower edge of each sheep's face. Smooth into shape with a hot brush, as in Step 2.

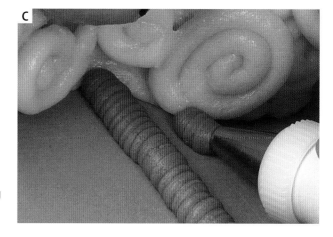

tip

If you are not partial to buttercream, use sugarpaste and a sugar shaper fitted with a small round disc to pipe the swirls and legs, then use balls of modelling paste for the sheep's heads and ears.

Perky Parrots

What could be better for a children's pirate party than these jolly parrot-topped cupcakes. With their dazzling colours, they are bound to make an awesome display in the centre of the table.

The parrots' heads are formed by using just the upper part of a parrot mould and then painted using paste colours diluted with clear spirit. But this painting project doesn't require a great deal of precision, and you can use whatever colours you like, as long as they are suitably vivid.

you will need ...

materials

- 270g (9 1/2oz) white modelling paste
- paste colours: yellow, red/orange, black
- clear spirit, such as gin or vodka
- 24 lemon or other flavoured cupcakes, or chocolate cupcakes
- complementary flavour of syrup, alcohol, buttercream or ganache
- 650g (1lb 7oz) blue sugarpaste (rolled fondant)
- sugar glue (see Sugar Recipes)

equipment

- parrot mould (DP)
- paint palette
- paintbrushes
- non-stick work board
- large and small rolling pin
- 5mm (³⁄₁₆in) spacers
- circle cutter same diameter as top of cupcakes
- palette knife

Making the parrots' heads

1 Knead the modelling paste to make it warm and pliable. Place a marble-sized ball of the paste in the head of the parrot mould. Firmly press the paste into the mould and then release it. Repeat to make 24 parrots' heads in total.

2 Using a paint palette, separately dilute each paste colour with clear spirit. Paint each parrot head with the paste colours applied with paintbrushes, following the photo as a guide (see Painting Techniques). Leave to dry completely.

Making and finishing the cupcakes

1 Make and bake your chosen flavour of cupcakes (see Baking Cupcakes for recipes).

2 Brush the cakes with syrup or alcohol or add a thin layer of buttercream or ganache (see Sugar Recipes), to help keep them fresh and to help the sugarpaste stick to the cakes.

3 Knead the sugarpaste to warm, then roll out between the 5mm (³⁄₁₆in) spacers, ideally on a non-stick surface. Cut out 24 circles using a circle cutter of the appropriate size. Using a palette knife, carefully lift each paste circle onto a cupcake. Attach a parrot's head to each cupcake with sugar glue.

Teddy Bears' Picnic

Teddies are always popular, with adults as well as children,
and these little chaps are very endearing, each with his own
little picnic rug laid out on a circle of lush green grass.

These lovable bears taste as good as they look, since they are made from
delicious dairy fudge, and using a mould set means that you get bears in a
variety of poses. The grass effect is achieved by texturing the sugarpaste with a
pan scourer, and a square of red modelling paste is repeatedly cut with a craft
knife around the edges to create a convincing fringed border.

you will need ...

materials

- 24 lemon or other flavoured cupcakes, or chocolate cupcakes
- complementary flavour of syrup, alcohol, buttercream or ganache
- 650g (1lb 7oz) green sugarpaste (rolled fondant)
- 120g (4¼oz) red modelling paste
- 1 packet dairy fudge
- sugar glue (see Sugar Recipes)
- small amount of buttercream
- black paste colour

equipment

- non-stick work board
- large and small rolling pin
- 5mm (³⁄₁₆in) spacers
- cutters: circle cutter same diameter as top of cupcakes; 4cm (1½in) square cutter (FMM geometric set)
- palette knife
- 2 pan scourers with different textures
- narrow spacers made from 1.5mm (¹⁄₁₆in) thick card
- craft knife
- straightedge
- teddy mould (DP Teddy Bears' Picnic)
- reusable piping (pastry) bag
- no. 1 piping tube (tip)

Making and preparing the cupcakes

1 Make and bake your chosen flavour of cupcakes (see Baking Cupcakes for recipes).

2 Brush the cakes with syrup or alcohol or add a thin layer of buttercream or ganache (see Sugar Recipes), to help keep them fresh and to help the sugarpaste stick to the cakes.

3 Knead the sugarpaste to warm, then roll out between the 5mm (³⁄₁₆in) spacers, ideally on a non-stick surface. Cut out 24 circles using a circle cutter of the appropriate size. Using a palette knife, carefully lift each paste circle onto a cupcake.

4 Take one pan scourer and firmly press it into the soft sugarpaste to create a grass-like texture (A).

A

Making the rugs

1 Roll out the red modelling paste between the narrow spacers. Use the 4cm (1½in) square cutter to cut out 24 squares. Mark a narrow border along all four sides of each square, with the lines intersecting at the corners, then use a craft knife to fringe the border, leaving the corners unfringed (B). Cut away the corners.

2 Texture the rugs with the other pan scourer, then lay a finished rug on the centre of each cupcake.

B

Creating the teddies

1 Knead the dairy fudge until warm. Press a small portion into each of the separate moulds in the teddy mould set and then release. Repeat to make 24 teddies in total. For some of the teddies, bend their legs forwards from the hip so that they can sit on their cupcakes. Allow the fudge teddies to firm up slightly before attaching to the centre of each rug with sugar glue.

2 Colour the small amount of buttercream black with black paste colour. Place the buttercream in a reusable piping bag fitted with a no. 1 piping tube and pipe eyes onto each teddy.

Mini Picnic

To complete the teddy bears' picnic scene, why not bake some mini cupcakes to intersperse among the teddy cupcakes.

1 Decorate by piping chocolate ganache of a piping consistency or chocolate buttercream (see Sugar Recipes) with a large star tube.

2 Top each piped mini cupcake in the centre with a bright yellow sweet (candy) of your choice.

Sea Scenes

Conjure up the relaxing and delightful experience of swimming
in warm, tropical, turquoise waters surrounded by fascinating
and beautiful fish, with this unusual collection of cupcakes.

Templates are provided for cutting out the fish bodies and fins (see
Templates), then their colours are enhanced with a little painted-on paste
colour. The watery effect is created by applying and subtly swirling a wash
of turquoise paste colour onto pale blue sugarpaste. For the finishing touch,
droplets of warmed piping gel are dotted around to look like bubbles.

you will need ...

materials

- 24 lemon or other flavoured cupcakes, or chocolate cupcakes
- complementary flavour of syrup, alcohol, buttercream or ganache
- 650g (1lb 7oz) pale blue sugarpaste (rolled fondant)
- paste colours: turquoise, blue, green
- clear spirit, such as gin or vodka
- white vegetable fat (shortening)
- modelling paste: 50g (1¾oz) pale blue; 25g (1oz) each green, cream, black
- sugar glue (see Sugar Recipes)
- small quantity of royal icing
- piping gel

equipment

- non-stick work board
- large and small rolling pin
- 5mm (³⁄₁₆in) spacers
- circle cutter same diameter as top of cupcakes
- palette knife
- flat-headed and fine paintbrushes
- narrow spacers made from 1.5mm (¹⁄₁₆in) thick card
- cutting wheel
- paint palette
- no. 1 piping tube (tip)
- reusable piping (pastry) bag

Making and preparing the cupcakes

1 Make and bake your chosen flavour of cupcakes (see Baking Cupcakes for recipes).

2 Brush the cakes with syrup or alcohol or add a thin layer of buttercream or ganache (see Sugar Recipes), to help keep them fresh and to help the sugarpaste stick to the cakes.

3 Knead the sugarpaste to warm, then roll out between the 5mm (³⁄₁₆in) spacers, ideally on a non-stick surface. Cut out 24 circles using a circle cutter of the appropriate size. Using a palette knife, carefully lift each paste circle onto a cupcake.

Creating the seawater background

1 Once the sugarpaste circles on top of the cupcakes are dry, weekly dilute some turquoise paste colour with clear spirit to make a wash. Using a flat-headed paintbrush, apply the wash in roughly parallel strokes across the sugarpaste discs (A). Then draw the tip of the paintbrush repeatedly through the wet wash in an overlapping wave action to create a subtle pattern (B). Leave to dry.

2 Add a subtle shine to the icing by painting over the sugarpaste with a layer of white vegetable fat. If using hard fat, melt it first before applying.

A

B

Making the fish designs

1 Roll out the pale blue modelling paste between the narrow spacers. Using the fish templates (see Templates), cut out six of each of the two different fish bodies, excluding the fins, with a cutting wheel. Use the cutting wheel to mark the gills on each fish. Place the bodies on the cupcakes, allowing sufficient space for the fins.

2 Knead the green modelling paste until warm, adding a little white vegetable fat and boiled water if necessary to make the paste elastic and workable, then roll out between the narrow spacers. Use the templates to cut around the outside lines of the fins and tails for each of the two fish with the cutting wheel, again cutting six sets of each.

3 Use the cutting wheel to mark the fins and tail pieces (C). Then attach the fins and tail pieces in place on the appropriate cupcakes.

C

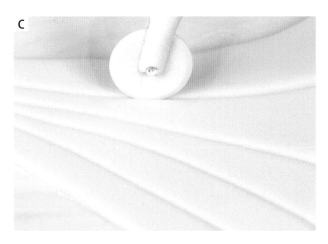

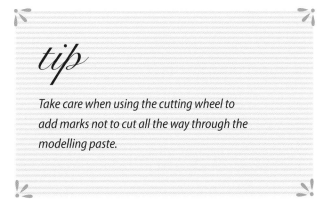

tip

Take care when using the cutting wheel to add marks not to cut all the way through the modelling paste.

4 Use a paint palette to dilute some turquoise, blue and green paste colour separately with clear spirit. Using a paintbrush, paint over each fish, applying a stronger colour over the back of the fishes and painting the underside with a more dilute colour.

5 Apply strokes of diluted green paste colour to the fins, using a darker colour at the ends of the fins and a lighter one where the fins will meet the body (C). Blend the colours with a damp paintbrush and then leave to dry.

tip

If you wish to darken the colour of your fish painting, wait until the surface is dry and then paint over another coat.

6 For the eyes, roll small balls of cream modelling paste and attach one to each fish. Roll smaller balls of black modelling paste and add as pupils, positioning them slightly off-centre. Put a small amount of royal icing into a piping bag fitted with a no. 1 tube and pipe a tiny light dot onto each pupil.

Adding the bubbles

Warm some piping gel in a microwave or a heatproof bowl set over a saucepan of simmering water until the gel is lump-free. Load a paintbrush with the gel and carefully place droplets of varying sizes onto the cupcakes without the fish. Add a few small droplets emerging from the mouths of the fish.

tip

You could change the colour of the fish to reds and oranges for goldfish or a selection of bright colours to look like tropical fish.

Stunning Starfish

These eye-catching starfish cupcakes instantly evoke carefree
sunny days spent on the beach, so they are the perfect choice for
an informal high summer celebration, whether it's a birthday party
or just a friends and family get-together around the barbecue.

This is a suitably simple, laid-back project to match the mood of the occasion,
using a commercial mould to make the starfish shapes. These are then enhanced
with a coat of orange paste colour diluted with orange paste colour. Job done!

you will need …

materials

- 24 lemon or other flavoured cupcakes, or chocolate cupcakes
- complementary flavour of syrup, alcohol, buttercream or ganache
- 650g (1lb 7oz) bright blue sugarpaste (rolled fondant)
- 25g (1oz) orange modelling paste
- orange paste colour
- clear spirit, such as gin or vodka
- sugar glue (see Sugar Recipes)

equipment

- non-stick work board
- large and small rolling pin
- 5mm (³⁄₁₆in) spacers
- circle cutter same diameter as top of cupcakes
- palette knife
- starfish mould (DP Large Seashore)
- paintbrush

Making and preparing the cupcakes

1 Make and bake your chosen flavour of cupcakes (see Baking Cupcakes for recipes).

2 Brush the cakes with syrup or alcohol or add a thin layer of buttercream or ganache (see Sugar Recipes), to help keep them fresh and to help the sugarpaste stick to the cakes.

3 Knead the sugarpaste to warm, then roll out between the 5mm (³⁄₁₆in) spacers, ideally on a non-stick surface. Cut out 24 circles using a circle cutter of the appropriate size. Using a palette knife, carefully lift each paste circle onto a cupcake.

Making the starfish decorations

1 Knead the orange modelling paste until warm. Roll five thin sausages of the paste, place one sausage in each arm of the starfish mould and press down firmly. Cut off any excess paste from the back of the mould and release. Repeat to make a total of 24 starfish.

2 Dilute some orange paste colour with clear spirit. Paint over the starfish with a paintbrush and leave to dry.

3 Once dry, attach a starfish to the centre of each cupcake with sugar glue.

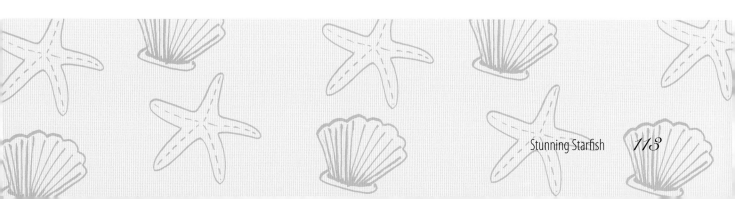

Terrific Tortoises

These friendly faced tortoise cupcakes are a fun, quirky idea for a
children's party, or would make a novel gift for an ardent pet-lover.
Their warm orangy-brown tones add to their inviting nature.

This project involves making your own mould, which is straightforward to
accomplish by following the detailed instructions given in the Making Moulds
section. Then you can enjoy the task of painting on the tortoises' shell markings
and creating a scale-like effect for their heads and feet, to make them realistic.

you will need …

materials

- 24 lemon or other flavoured cupcakes, or chocolate cupcakes
- complementary flavour of syrup, alcohol, buttercream or ganache
- paste colours: golden brown (Spectral – Autumn Leaf), violet, mid-orange (SK – Marigold), dark orange (SK – Nasturtium)
- 650g (1lb 7oz) golden brown sugarpaste (rolled fondant)
- non-toxic modelling clay or Plasticine, available from toy and art stores
- pot of moulding gel
- 250g (9oz) orange modelling paste
- clear spirit, such as gin or vodka
- edible white dust colour
- sugar glue (see Sugar Recipes)

equipment

- non-stick work board
- large and small rolling pin
- 5mm (³⁄₁₆in) spacers
- circle cutter same diameter as top of cupcakes
- palette knife
- Dresden tool
- cutting wheel
- paintbrushes and stippling brush

Making and preparing the cupcakes

1 Make and bake your chosen flavour of cupcakes (see Baking Cupcakes for recipes).

2 Brush the cakes with syrup or alcohol or add a thin layer of buttercream or ganache (see Sugar Recipes), to help keep them fresh and to help the sugarpaste stick to the cakes.

3 Knead the sugarpaste to warm, then roll out between the 5mm (³⁄₁₆in) spacers, ideally on a non-stick surface. Cut out 24 circles using a circle cutter of the appropriate size. Using a palette knife, carefully lift each paste circle onto a cupcake.

Moulding the tortoises

Follow the instructions in the Making Moulds section to make your own tortoise mould from non-toxic clay or Plasticine and then use it to form 24 tortoises from the orange modelling paste.

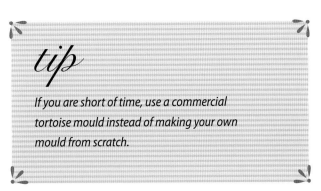

tip

If you are short of time, use a commercial tortoise mould instead of making your own mould from scratch.

Painting the tortoises

1 Slightly dilute the paste colours separately with clear spirit in a paint palette. Mix a dark brown by combining the golden brown and violet paste colours together, then mix a light purple-brown by combining the edible white dust colour with violet and some of the dark brown colour you have just mixed.

2 Using a fine paintbrush, paint lines of the light purple-brown colour between each section of the shell to help emphasize the pattern markings.

3 Paint the outer portion of each shell section with the dark brown colour. Change the brush and paint over the centre of the shell sections with mid-orange and then around the edges with dark orange.

4 Use the orange colour to paint tiny circles over the head and feet to resemble scales, or use a stippling brush to create a textured effect.

5 Paint on the tortoise's mouth and eye with the dark brown paste colour.

6 Paint the remaining tortoises in the same way and leave to dry completely, then attach one to the centre of each cupcake with sugar glue.

Safari Stars

This delightful collection of animal cupcakes gathers together and celebrates the big, beautiful beasts of the wild. Everyone's favourites are here to enjoy, including the panda, tiger, hippo and elephant.

You get a lot for your money with a single set of animal cutters, used here to cut out this host of fabulous animals. Then you and the children can have fun choosing which ones to group together to make a mini safari scene. You can even use small elements of a cut-out, like the head of the giraffe popping out behind the hippo! Once your animals are in place, really make them come alive by highlighting their markings and defining features with diluted paste colours.

you will need . . .

materials

- 24 lemon or other flavoured cupcakes, or chocolate cupcakes
- complementary flavour of syrup, alcohol, buttercream or ganache
- 650g (1lb 7 oz) lime green sugarpaste (rolled fondant)
- modelling paste: 50g (1¾oz) each orange, yellow, grey, brown, white
- sugar glue (see Sugar Recipes)
- paste colours: black, brown, red
- clear spirit, such as gin or vodka

equipment

- non-stick work board
- large and small rolling pin
- 5mm (³⁄₁₆in) spacers
- cutters: circle cutter same diameter as top of cupcakes; animal cutters (FMM Safari Animal set)
- palette knife
- narrow spacers made from 1.5mm (¹⁄₁₆in) thick card
- paint palette
- paintbrushes

Making and preparing the cupcakes

1 Make and bake your chosen flavour of cupcakes (see Baking Cupcakes for recipes).

2 Brush the cakes with syrup or alcohol or add a thin layer of buttercream or ganache (see Sugar Recipes), to help keep them fresh and to help the sugarpaste stick to the cakes.

3 Knead the sugarpaste to warm, then roll out between the 5mm (³⁄₁₆in) spacers, ideally on a non-stick surface. Cut out 24 circles using a circle cutter of the appropriate size. Using a palette knife, carefully lift each paste circle onto a cupcake.

Making the animal decorations

1 Roll out the modelling paste colours between the narrow spacers. Use the animal cutters to cut out a variety of animal shapes from the appropriate-coloured paste: place the paste over the Tappit cutters, roll over the paste with a rolling pin, then run a finger around the top of the cutter to achieve a clean cut. Tap the cutter on the work surface to release the paste shape. You will need at least 72 in total. Attach mixed groups of three animals to the centre of each cupcake with sugar glue.

2 Dilute the paste colours separately with clear spirit in a paint palette. Using paintbrushes, paint each animal to enhance its markings, referring to the photo as a guide.

Tiger Treats

These unusual cupcakes are sure to be a hit with wildlife lovers of every age, and are great for an eco-themed party. They will give you the ideal opportunity to showcase your painting talents, but the effect is actually quite straightforward to create following the step-by-step instructions and photos – especially the 'furry' designs. The secret of success is to work slowly and stop every so often to stand back and check how the painting looks.

You could easily alter the markings to make jaguar, cheetah or leopard heads and fur, using a suitable picture as a reference.

you will need ...

materials

- 24 lemon or other flavoured cupcakes, or chocolate cupcakes
- complementary flavour of syrup, alcohol, buttercream or ganache
- sugarpaste (rolled fondant): 325g (11½oz) each green, white
- non-toxic modelling clay or Plasticine
- pot of moulding gel
- white modelling paste
- paste colours: golden brown (Spectral – Autumn Leaf), black, pink
- clear spirit, such as gin or vodka
- sugar glue (see Sugar Recipes)

equipment

- large and small rolling pin
- 5mm (³⁄₁₆in) spacers
- circle cutter same diameter as top of cupcakes
- palette knife
- Dresden tool
- cutting wheel
- soft medium and fine paintbrushes

Making and preparing the cupcakes

1 Make and bake your chosen flavour of cupcakes (see Baking Cupcakes for recipes).

2 Brush the cakes with syrup or alcohol or add a thin layer of buttercream or ganache (see Sugar Recipes), to help keep them fresh and to help the sugarpaste stick to the cakes.

3 Knead the green sugarpaste to warm, then roll out between the 5mm (³⁄₁₆in) spacers, ideally on a non-stick surface. Cut out 12 circles using a circle cutter of the appropriate size. Using a palette knife, carefully lift each paste circle onto a cupcake.

Making the tiger's head design

1 Make a mould for the tiger's head, following the instructions in the Making Moulds section, using modelling clay or Plasticine and moulding gel.

2 Using white modelling paste and your mould, make 12 tigers' heads, again following the instructions in the Making Moulds section (A).

3 Dilute some golden brown paste colour with clear spirit and, using a soft medium paintbrush, apply to the tiger's head (B). Leave to dry completely.

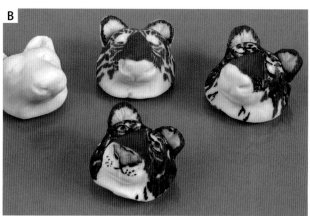

4 Dilute the black paste colour with clear spirit just enough to make it painting consistency, then, using a fine paintbrush, apply the distinctive tiger's markings, including the outlining of the eyes (B). Again, leave to dry completely.

5 Paint in the tiger's nose using clear spirit-diluted pink paste colour, then complete the eyes by adding the irises in golden brown and finally black pupils (B).

6 Repeat for the remaining tigers' heads, then attach one to each of the green-covered cupcakes with sugar glue.

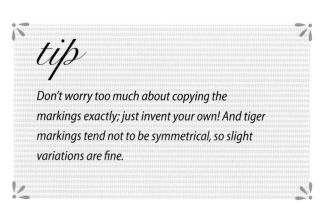

tip

Don't worry too much about copying the markings exactly; just invent your own! And tiger markings tend not to be symmetrical, so slight variations are fine.

Making the tiger fur design

1 Knead the white sugarpaste to warm, then roll out between the 5mm (³⁄₁₆in) spacers, ideally on a non-stick surface. Cut out 12 circles using a circle cutter of the appropriate size. Texture using a cutting wheel by running the wheel repeatedly through the paste in one direction only, taking care not to cut all the way through the paste, except on the edges of the circles (C). Use a palette knife to carefully lift each textured paste circle onto the remaining uncovered cupcakes.

2 Dilute the golden brown paste colour with clear spirit and paint in some stripes across the textured sugarpaste (D). Leave to dry completely, then add the black markings, ensuring that your paste colour isn't too thin, otherwise it may run. Also make sure that you leave a few areas of the sugarpaste white. .

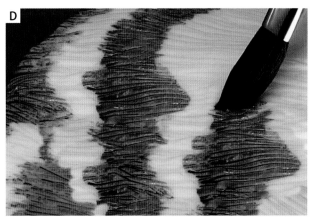

tip

If you make a mistake with your painting, you can carefully remove a small area with a dampened flat-headed paintbrush.

Abbreviations & Equivalents

g = grams

oz = ounces (1oz = 30g approx)

cm = centimetres (1cm = 3/8in approx)

mm = millimetres

in = inches (1in = 2.5cm approx)

ml = millilitres

tsp = teaspoon (1tsp = 5ml)

tbsp = tablespoon (1tbsp =15ml)

fl = fluid ounces

US Cup Measurements

If you prefer to use cup measurements, please use the following conversions. (Note: Australian cup measurements are slightly larger than US cup measurements. 1 Australian tbsp = 20ml.)

liquid

½ cup = 120ml (4fl oz)

1 cup = 240ml (8fl oz)

butter

1tbsp = 15g (½oz)

2tbsp = 25g (1oz)

½ cup/1 stick = 115g (4oz)

1 cup/2 sticks = 225g (8oz)

caster (superfine) sugar

½ cup = 100g (3½oz)

1 cup = 200g (7oz)

icing (confectioners')sugar

1 cup = 115g (4oz)

Equivalent Terms

UK	US
black treacle	blackstrap molasses
bicarbonate of soda	baking soda
cake tin	cake pan
caster sugar	superfine sugar
cling film	plastic wrap
CMC powder	Tylose powder
cocktail stick	toothpick
cocoa powder	unsweetened cocoa
cornflour	cornstarch
currants	small raisins
glacé cherries	candied cherries
greaseproof paper	wax paper
icing sugar	confectioners' sugar
mixed peel	candied citrus peel
mixed spice	apple pie spice
plain flour	all-purpose flour
self-raising flour	self-rising flour
soft brown sugar	light brown sugar
sugarpaste	rolled fondant icing
sultanas	golden raisins
white vegetable fat	shortening

Templates

Sea Scenes

Crowning Glory

Suppliers

UK

Lindy's Cakes Ltd (LC)
Unit 2
Station Approach
Wendover
Bucks
HP22 6BN
Tel: +44 (0)1296 622418
www.lindyscakes.co.uk
Manufacturer of cutters plus online
shop for equipment used in this and
Lindy's other books

Knightbridge PME Ltd (W)
Chadwell Heath Lane
Romford
Essex
RN6 4NP
Tel: +44 (0)20 8590 5959
www.cakedecoration.co.uk
UK distributor of Wilton products

M&B Specialised Confectioners Ltd
3a Millmead Estate
Mill Mead road
London
N17 9ND
Tel: +44 (0)20 8801 7948
www.mbsc.co.uk
Manufacturers and suppliers of sugarpaste

US

Global Sugar Art, LLC
625 Route 3
Unit 3
Plattsburgh
NY 12901
Tel: 518 561 3039
www.globalsugarart.com
Sugarcraft supplier that imports
many UK products to the US

Wilton Industries, Inc. (W)
2240 West 75th Street
Woodridge
1L 60517
United States
Tel (Retail Customer orders):
+1 800 794 5866
www.wilton.com

Australia

Iced Affair
53 Church Street
Camperdown
NSW 2050
Tel: (02) 9519 3679
www.icedaffair.com.au
Sugarcraft supplier

Key to abbreviations:

DP	Diamond Paste and	LC	Lindy's Cakes Ltd
	Mould Co	PC	Patchwork Cutters
FMM	FMM Sugarcraft	SK	Squire's Kitchen
HP	Holly Products	T	Tinkertech Two
JEM	JEM Cutters cc	W	Wilton Industries Inc

About the Author

Well known, and highly respected in the Sugarcraft industry, Lindy Smith has over 20 years experience in sugarcrafting. Lindy is a designer, who likes to share her love of sugarcraft and inspire fellow enthusiasts by writing books and teaching. Lindy is the author of nine cake decorating titles for D&C: *Creative Celebration Cakes, Storybook Cakes, Celebrate with a Cake!, Party Animal Cakes, Cakes to Inspire and Desire, Bake Me I'm Yours... Cookie, Bake Me I'm Yours... Cupcake, Celebrate with Mini Cakes* and *The Contemporary Cake Decorating Bible*.

Lindy's teaching takes her all around the world, giving her the opportunity to educate and inspire whilst also learning about local traditions and cake decorating issues. This knowledge is ultimately then fed back into her work. She has also appeared on television in programmes such as *The Generation Game* and presented a sugarcraft series on *Good Food Live*.

Lindy also heads Lindy's Cakes Ltd, a well-established business that runs her online shop www.lindyscakes.co.uk, and her cake decorating workshops both in the UK and abroad. To see what Lindy is currently doing, become a fan of Lindy's Cakes on Facebook or follow Lindy on Twitter. For baking advice and a wealth of information visit her blog, via the Lindy's Cakes website: www.lindyscakes.co.uk.

Index

Recipe Notes